FOLLOWING MARY TO JESUS

OUR LADY AS
MOTHER, TEACHER, AND ADVOCATE

ANDREW APOSTOLI, CFR

Published by The Word Among Us Press
9639 Doctor Perry Road
Ijamsville, Maryland 21754
www.wordamongus.org

12 11 10 09 08 1 2 3 4 5

ISBN: 978-1-59325-118–5

Unless otherwise noted, Scripture passages contained herein are from the
New Revised Standard Version Bible: Catholic Edition, © 1989, 1993,
Division of Christian Education of the National Council of the Churches
of Christ in the United States. All rights reserved. Used with permission.
Scripture texts marked RSV taken from the Revised Standard Version:
Catholic edition, © 1965 and 1966, Division of Christian Education of
the National Council of the Churches of Christ in the United States. All
rights reserved. Used with permission.
Scripture texts marked NAB are from the New American Bible with
Revised New Testament and Revised Psalms, © 1991, 1986, 1970,
Confraternity of Christian Doctrine, Washington, D.C., and are used by
permission of the copyright owner. All rights reserved. No part of the
New American Bible maybe reproduced in any form without permission
in writing from the copyright owner.

Cover design by John Hamilton Design
Puligo, Domenico (1492-1527) Madonna and Child with Two Angels
Location: Galleria Borghese, Rome, Italy
Photo Credi: Scala/Art Resource, NY

Made and printed in the United States of America

Library of Congress Cataloging-in-Publication Data

Apostoli, Andrew.
  Following Mary to Jesus : Our Lady as mother, teacher, and advocate /
Andrew Apostoli.
     p. cm.
  ISBN 978-1-59325-118-5 (alk. paper)
  1. Mary, Blessed Virgin, Saint. I. Title.
  BT603.A66 2008
  232.91--dc22
                                    2008032195

Contents

INTRODUCTION

Before his conversion to the Catholic Church, Cardinal John Henry Newman (d. 1890) undertook a study aimed at showing that the Anglican Church was the true Church as Christ had founded it and that the Roman Catholic Church had actually changed the Lord's original teachings. What he discovered brought him to the very opposite conclusion and initiated his conversion to Catholicism.

What Newman discovered about Mary was of particular interest. When he delved into the writings of the Fathers of the Church of the first and second centuries, he found that the theology about Mary was the same then as it was in his own time (and still is now)! For example, he discovered that St. Irenaeus (d. 202) referred to her as the "New Eve." He found evidence of Mary's important role in the mysteries of the incarnation and the redemption. The only difference, he discovered, was a significant growth in devotion to Mary, especially from the time of St. Bernard of Clairvaux (d. 1153) and St. Francis of Assisi (d. 1226). This devotion stressed her role as intercessor and protectress in times of sickness, war, plague, and heresy. This in turn corresponded with a growth in devotion to the humanity of Jesus with a stress on his poverty, humility, and sufferings.

Another interesting insight Newman discovered was that whenever there was correct teaching about Mary, there was usually correct teaching about Jesus. But whenever there was distorted or false teaching about Mary, there was always false or distorted teaching about Jesus.

What emerged from Cardinal Newman's research were two important truths concerning Our Lady. The first is that Mary played an immensely important role in the saving mission of her divine Son. She continues to play an important role in the redemption of the world by helping to dispense to all her children the merits and blessings that Jesus won for us. The second truth is that a true devotion to Our Lady is one of the surest ways to remain faithful to authentic Church teachings.

In these perilous times in which we live, Mary's part in God's plan for the peace of the world and the salvation of souls is increasingly evident. Her message at Fatima, as Pope John Paul II said after the attempt on his life on May 13, 1981, is more important today than it was in 1917. Recognizing Mary's crucial role in our lives is essential to our ability to cooperate as fully as we can with God's plan for our times.

Many saints, like St. Alphonsus Mary Liguori (d. 1787) and St. Louis Marie Grignon de Montfort (d. 1716), considered devotion to Mary to be a sign of God's special predilection. To be close to Our Lady is, after all, the surest way to be close to Jesus. Too many of us, though, don't appreciate the role Mary can play in our lives. This book focuses on three ways in which Our Lady is ready to help us every day: as our mother, our teacher, and our advocate. Mary brought life to Jesus, and as our mother, she continues to bring life to all of us, her spiritual children. As our teacher, Mary helps us learn to trust in God's providential working in our lives in the same way that she completely abandoned herself to his will in her own life. And as our advocate, Mary shows us compassion and always answers our prayers, preparing our hearts to receive the mercy God wants to give us.

Our Lady is extending a loving hand to each of us to lead us on our spiritual journey. All we need to do is take her hand and follow her to Jesus.

Part One

OUR MOTHER

MARY BRINGS LIFE TO HER CHILDREN

In a beautiful prayer he composed in honor of the Blessed Virgin Mary, St. Francis of Assisi noted the greatness and uniqueness of Our Lady among all women:

> Holy, Virgin Mary, there is no one like you among all the women in the world.
> You are the daughter and the handmaid of the most high supreme King and Father of heaven.
> You are the mother of our most holy lord Jesus Christ.
> You are the spouse of the Holy Spirit.
> Pray for us with Saint Michael the archangel and all the powers of the heavens and the saints to your most holy beloved Son, Lord and Master.[1]

Our Lady is absolutely unique among all God's creatures, because she stands in a special relationship to the Most Holy Trinity. She is the loving daughter of God the Father. She is the loving mother of God the Son. She is the loving spouse of God the Holy Spirit.

She is also our mother. Why? Because she gave birth to Jesus, who came to bring us the fullness of life. Since Mary joined with Jesus so intimately in his redemptive work, she is a mother bringing life to all of her children. She is the true Eve, or "mother of the living," being both the mother of the whole Church and, in a very personal way, a mother to each of us.

CHAPTER I

The Holy Spirit, Giver of Life

Mary became our spiritual mother through the working of the Holy Spirit. Unfortunately, many Catholics know so little about him that he is sometimes referred to as "the forgotten God." This is largely because his mission is hidden in the depths of our hearts and his nature is rather mysterious. For example, we know what a human father is, and therefore we can somewhat relate to God the Father. We know what a human son is, which helps us relate to God the Son. But it is hard for us to imagine what a spirit is, and so we find it is more difficult to grasp God the Holy Spirit.

THE GIVER OF LIFE AT THE FIRST CREATION

In the Nicene Creed, we call the Holy Spirit "the Lord, the Giver of life." Interestingly, the Old Testament account of the creation at the beginning of time says that a "mighty wind" swept over a barren wasteland and an abyss of lifeless waters (see Genesis 1:1-2). The Hebrew word for wind, *ruah*, can actually mean "wind" or "breath" or "spirit." For the ancient Hebrew people, there was a connection among these three elements. "Wind" was a rather mysterious flowing of air, while "breath" was the air that came in and out of a person, and "spirit" was the living air or breath within a person. We can see this in the Genesis account of creation that states that after God formed the body of Adam, he breathed air into Adam. At that point, Adam received the breath of life and became a living being. This breath of life in Adam was his spirit.

So if we look again at the statement that a "mighty wind" swept over the wasteland and the abyss, we can actually translate "mighty wind" as the "spirit of God." For the ancient Hebrew people, the spirit of God meant his power, which was creative and life-giving. Therefore, we can understand the creation story at the beginning of time as an effect of God's life-giving spirit or power coming over or overshadowing a wasteland and an abyss that were empty and void, lifeless and formless. The wasteland was virgin land. But when the spirit of God overshadowed this wasteland, it became capable of bearing life. In fact, it became fruitful. Trees and vegetation grew on the land. Animals lived on it, too. The same happened to the waters of the abyss. These waters, drained from the land to form the seas, teemed with fish.

For the Jewish people, then, spirit would have referred to one of God's qualities or attributes. It would have meant his power. They would not have understood spirit to mean the Holy Spirit, the third divine Person of the blessed Trinity, as we now understand it in light of the revelation of the New Testament.

The Giver of Life at the New Creation

Later, as described in Luke's Gospel, there is a new or second creation when the archangel Gabriel appeared to Mary at the Annunciation. Referring to baptism and its effect upon us, St. Paul said that we are made into a new creation (see 2 Corinthians 5:17). This second creation began not at the beginning of time, but in what St. Paul called the "fullness of time" (Galatians 4:4).

In this "fullness of time" at the Annunciation, the Holy Spirit overshadowed Mary. She was a virgin and would remain a virgin. She was "espoused," or solemnly betrothed, to Joseph, but St. Luke tells us that before they came to live together, she was told by the archangel that she would have a Son. Our Lady then questioned the angel, "How shall this happen since I do not know man?" Mary's question indicates not only that she has not been with Joseph as his wife, but also implies that she will remain a virgin even after they come to live together. The archangel's response clarifies God's plan: "The Holy Spirit shall overshadow you, so that the child born of you will be the Son of the Most High" (see Luke 1:34-35).

> When the fullness of time had come, God sent his Son, born of a woman, born under the law, in order to redeem those who were under the law, so that we might receive adoption as children.
>
> —Galatians 4:4-5

As the Spirit of God swept over the virgin land in the Old Testament at the first creation and made it fruitful, now in the New Testament, at the beginning of a new creation, the Spirit of God overshadows the Virgin Mary, and she brings forth life in her womb. In fact, Mary brought forth the very author and source of life itself.

The birth of Jesus is the greatest act of love the world has ever seen—God becoming man, one of us. On God's side, this meant three things: that the Father would love us so much that he would send his only Son to be our savior; that the Son would love us so much that he would lay down his life for us in the cruel suffering of the cross; and that the Holy Spirit would love us so much that he would bring about the incarnation of the Word.

But there also had to be an incredible act of love on the part of mankind to receive God's infinite love and to respond to it appropriately. Mary's loving response at the Annunciation, seen in her act of total self-surrender, was precisely what God awaited. Love is measured by giving, and Mary gave herself completely, unreservedly, and joyfully to God's plan. Mary was completely open to the will of God. In her self-abandonment, she called herself "the handmaid of the Lord," ready to do whatever the Lord would ask of her. She gave her total consent: "Let it be done to me according to your word" (Luke 1:38). This allowed the Holy Spirit to bring forth the fullness of life in Mary in the person of Jesus Christ.

CHRIST WAS CONCEIVED SPIRITUALLY
IN MARY'S HEART THROUGH THE HOLY SPIRIT

Mary actually conceived Jesus twice through the working of the Holy Spirit. St. Augustine tells us that before Christ was ever conceived physically in Mary's womb, he was already conceived spiritually in her heart. This presence of Christ was the result of grace. Mary had such a fullness of faith and love that the Lord was already living and dwelling in her spiritually.

St. Paul refers to this same spiritual indwelling of Christ in himself: "I live, no longer I, but Christ lives in me" (Galatians 2:20, NAB). The apostle then adds that he goes on living his human life but at the same time now lives a new life hidden with Christ in God; on the last day, this new life will be made visible. We also live this hidden life in faith, with Christ dwelling within us. This is why St. Paul also exhorts us to let Christ "dwell in your hearts through faith" (Ephesians 3:17) and to let "the word of Christ dwell in you richly" (Colossians 3:16). Because Mary was completely open to that word, the Word made flesh was already living in her spiritually.

If you look at a medieval painting of the Annunciation, you will probably notice a scroll or open book near Mary, containing the word of God. We can be sure that even before the Annunciation, Mary was already pondering God's word, the Scriptures, deeply in her heart. After all, she didn't have original sin or personal sin to block her understanding. Jesus, the eternal Word coming from the Father, was already spoken about prophetically in the Old Testament. As St. Augustine observed, Jesus already lay hidden in the pages of the Old Testament and was finally revealed in the pages of the New Testament. Through his incarnation in Mary, Jesus, the eternal Word, actually took on flesh and lived among us.

CHRIST WAS CONCEIVED PHYSICALLY IN MARY BY THE HOLY SPIRIT

The receptivity of Mary's heart opened her to the second way the Holy Spirit brought forth the Lord through her: by her conceiving Christ physically in her womb. As we have seen, St. Paul described that moment as the "fullness of time." It was a mysterious time, known only in the heart of God. What was this moment?

Perhaps we can offer one possible explanation. Among the Israelites in Old Testament times, there was a belief that if all the Jewish faithful at any one moment fervently yearned for the Messiah to come, he would indeed have come precisely at that moment. Why? Because the longing, the desire for the Messiah to come, would have reached its "fullness." So we may say that somehow the great longing in the heart of Our Lady for the fulfillment of God's promises represented that "fullness" of loving desire for the Messiah to come, and so he came!

St. Teresa of Ávila encourages us to have great desires in the spiritual life. We can't possibly imagine Mary having tiny desires. She had an incredibly burning desire to love God, to anticipate and hasten his work in the world. Even St. Peter, writing about the second coming of Jesus, said that we should not only look forward to that coming, but should try to hasten it by yearning, by desiring the Lord to come (see 2 Peter 3:12). Christ will see that longing on the part of his people, and he will come. In the last verses of the Book of Revelation, St. John speaks of the Holy Spirit and "the bride," which is the Church, crying out, "Come, Lord Jesus!" (Revelation 22:20). The Church, inspired by the Holy Spirit, yearns for this second coming of Christ. In an earlier age, Mary longed for the fulfillment of God's promised Messiah, and in her the Word became flesh. The Son of God became the son of Mary. St. Francis of Assisi often told his friars that they should honor Mary because through her, the Lord of majesty became their brother.

We have already mentioned St. Paul's words in his Letter to the Galatians, "When the fullness of time had come, God sent his Son, born of a woman" (4:4). Many people have wondered why Paul didn't make it more personal by writing, "born of Mary." Pope John Paul II, in his letter on the dignity and role of women in the Church, noted that this word choice indicates the significance of God's entrusting the care of his Son to a woman (*Mulieres Dignitatem*, 3). You see, in Jesus' time, women not only physically cared for the children by feeding and clothing them but they also taught them the basics of the faith. Even today, according to the Jewish religion, if a Jewish person marries a Gentile, the religion of the child is always traced through the mother. So if the father is Jewish and the mother is Gentile, the child is considered a Gentile. But if the mother is Jewish, the child's religion is considered Judaism, because the mother raises the child in the faith. So not only does the mother initially give life but she also cares for that life, nourishes it, protects it, and lays the foundation for the spiritual life of her child.

As Pope John Paul II also suggested, Paul's use of the word "woman" is also significant because of Mary's relationship to the woman of Genesis—Eve—which we will see in the next chapter.

CHAPTER 2

Mary, Our Mother, Mediator of Life

Mary continues her role as mother of life with you and me and all of her spiritual children. As mother of Life himself, Mary mediates the life of Christ to us as the new Eve, as the Mother of the Church, and finally, as our mother.

THE NEW EVE

As the "woman" central to God's plan of salvation, Mary is the "new Eve." This is the very first title given to Mary in the writings of the Church fathers. St. Paul himself referred to Jesus as the "new Adam" (see Romans 5:14; 1 Corinthians 15:45). There is logic, then, in seeing Mary as the "new Eve" because of her role in giving life to all her spiritual children. We should also mention that the Church in a spiritual way is also called the "new Eve," because the Church is the mystical bride of Jesus, the Bridegroom, just as the first Eve was the spouse of the first Adam.

The name Eve means "the mother of the living" (see Genesis 3:20). But because the first Eve was joined to the sin of the first Adam, her sin passed on not life but death to her children. This death was both physical and spiritual. Physical death means the death of the body. Before the original sin, our first parents enjoyed the gift of immortality. Death, however, was a punishment for their sin which was passed on to all their descendents. The body would die by being separated from the soul. But even after the death of the body, the soul retains the hope of being reunited to the body at the time of the second coming of Jesus. Spiritual death means that we, as children of the first Eve, were born without the life of God's sanctifying grace in our souls. We could not redeem ourselves to gain back the life of grace we had lost because we couldn't pay the price of our own redemption. Unless something happened, the gates of heaven were closed to us forever!

> For Eve, being a virgin and undefiled, having conceived the word from the serpent, brought forth disobedience and death. The virgin Mary, however, having received faith and joy, when the angel Gabriel announced to her the good tidings . . . answered: "Be it done to me according to your word."
>
> —St. Justin Martyr (d. 165)

> Just as it was through a virgin who disobeyed [Eve] that mankind was stricken and fell and died, so too it was through the Virgin, who obeyed the word of God, that mankind, resuscitated by life, received life.
>
> —St. Irenaeus of Lyons (d. 200)

But Mary, as the new Eve, begins to reverse our helpless situation. She can do this because she is now joined to the redemptive work of her divine Son, the new Adam. Jesus came to bring us the fullness of life: "I came that they may have life, and have it abundantly" (John 10:10). Through his redemption, Jesus restores to us the life of grace that had been lost. This spiritual life is restored to the soul through baptism. At the same time, through his bodily resurrection, Jesus promises to raise our bodies back to life when he returns in glory at the end of time. Because Mary was joined to her Son's work so intimately, she is truly a mother who brings life to her spiritual children.

MOTHER OF THE CHURCH

As the new Eve, the true mother of the living, Mary is the Mother of the Church. St. Paul refers to the Church as the mystical body of Christ. Jesus is the head, while we who are baptized are the members (see Ephesians 5:23). Head and members make up the fullness of Christ's mystical body. In Bethlehem Mary gave birth to Jesus, our head.

On Calvary Mary became a mother again. Jesus addressed her as such when he said, "Woman, behold, your son" (John 19:26, NAB). To understand this mystical birth on Calvary, we have to look at the way John describes the death of Jesus. At dusk the Roman soldiers broke the legs of the two thieves crucified with Jesus. Breaking their legs hastened their deaths, because the only way to breathe on the cross was to lift oneself up by the legs to inhale. But when the soldiers came to Jesus, it was obvious that he was already dead. They did not break any of his bones, but to be sure that he was not alive, a centurion thrust his lance into

Jesus' side. John tells us that at that moment, blood and water came forth from the side of Christ (see John 19:31-34).

The early Church fathers saw this blood and water as symbols of the creation of the Church. Jesus is the new Adam. Mary is personally the new Eve, as the mother of the living members of Christ's mystical body. The Church is also the new Eve as the mystical spouse of Jesus, the new Adam. Just as the first Eve was formed from Adam's side in the garden of Eden, so the Church, as the new Eve, was formed from the side of Jesus on the cross at Calvary.

The Genesis creation account says that God put Adam into a deep sleep, opened his side, took out one of his ribs, and formed Eve (see Genesis 2:21-22). The Church fathers saw a parallel to the Genesis creation in the gospel account of Jesus' death. In their view, Jesus (the new Adam) was in the sleep of death on the cross, when his side was opened by the centurion's lance, and out came blood and water, symbolizing the Church. The water represents the Sacrament of Baptism, which gives us the beginning of new life in Christ; the blood represents the Eucharist, which gives us Christ himself, the very author of our new life. As the two greatest sacraments, Baptism and the Eucharist represent the Church itself.

Archbishop Fulton Sheen said that since the Church was mystically "born" from the side of Christ, there was a birth taking place, and so there had to be a mother. Mary was present at the cross and received from her divine Son a new role as mother of the living: "Woman, behold, your son" (John 19:26, NAB). *Woman*—Jesus again uses that title in addressing his mother, just as he did at the wedding at Cana. There was a deeper reason for his use of the word "woman," which we see when we look at Genesis. In the garden of Eden, God said to the serpent, who had just led the first Adam and the first Eve into sin,

> "I will put enmity between you and the woman,
>   and between your offspring and hers;
> he will strike your head,
>   and you will strike his heel."
> (Genesis 3:15)

When Jesus at Cana and again at Calvary called his mother "woman," we can conclude that he was identifying Mary as the one who would be at enmity with the evil one (the devil) and whose offspring would do battle with the devil's offspring.

When Jesus said to his mother as he was dying, "Woman, behold, your son," he was also identifying Mary as our mother. In giving life to Christ, who is our head, Mary gives us life also, since the same life that is in the head is also present in us who are the members of his mystical body.

Our Mother

St. Aelred of Rievaulx (d. 1167), a Cistercian abbot and a contemporary of St. Bernard of Clairvaux, explained Mary's role as our spiritual mother:

We owe [Mary] honor, for she is the mother of our Lord. He who fails to honor the mother clearly dishonors the Son. Also, Scripture says: *"Honor your father and your mother."* ...

Once we all lay in death, as you know and believe, in sin, in darkness, in misery. In death, because we had lost the Lord; in sin, because of our corruption; in darkness, for we were without the light of wisdom, and, thus had perished utterly.

But then we were born, far better than through Eve, through Mary the blessed [one], because Christ was born of her. We have recovered new life in place of sin, immortality instead of mortality, light in place of darkness.

She is our mother—the mother of our life [Jesus], the mother of our redemption [Jesus], the mother of our light [Jesus]. As the apostle [St. Paul] says of our Lord, *"He became for us, by God's power, our wisdom and justice, our holiness and redemption."*

[Mary] then, as mother of Christ, is the mother of our wisdom and justice, of our holiness and redemption. She is more our mother than the mother of our flesh. Our birth from her is better, for from her is born our holiness, our wisdom, our justice, our sanctification, our redemption.[2]

We all received new life in Christ, and Mary gave life to him by conceiving and giving birth to him. Therefore, we can say with

St. Aelred that Mary gave us life also, since we share in the very life Christ received from her. In the mystical body, the life that is in Jesus our head flows into us who are his members. This makes Mary's role for us one of being a mother of life. She is always spiritually mediating or transmitting life to us through and in Christ, who dwells within us.

Mary Brings Jesus to Us

How does Mary mediate life to us? First, she brings Jesus to us. Let's look at the visitation of Mary to her aged cousin, Elizabeth. The archangel Gabriel tells Mary that Elizabeth is with child. Hearing that news, Mary goes in haste to help her older cousin. When the women greet each other, Mary brings the grace and blessing of the Lord's presence to Elizabeth and to the child within her womb. Elizabeth acknowledges this, saying, "And who am I that the mother of my Lord should come to me? For as soon as I heard the sound of your greeting, the child in my womb leaped for joy" (see Luke 1:43-44).

The Church fathers said that at that precise moment, John the Baptist, while in his mother's womb, was freed of original sin and filled with grace. Mary was bringing the life-giving presence of Jesus to Elizabeth and to John. In response Mary burst forth into praise of God with her beautiful Magnificat: "My soul proclaims the greatness of the Lord; my spirit rejoices in God my Savior" (Luke 1:46-47, NAB). Mary became the mother who brings life, because she brings Jesus to us, as she did to St. Elizabeth and St. John the Baptist.

I once saw an unusual painting in a retreat house. It was an image of Our Lady enveloped completely in light. She had just traveled over a winding path, and the whole path was covered with light. At first I didn't understand what this meant, so I asked the resident priest to interpret it for me. He explained that the painting depicts Mary on her journey to see Elizabeth. Because Mary is carrying Christ within her, she is radiating the light of Christ wherever she goes. In the same way, she is bringing light and life to us by bringing Jesus to us.

Mary Obtains Faith for Us

Mary also helps us to find life because she obtains faith for us. In this regard, we look at the first miracle Jesus performed, at the wedding feast of Cana (see John 2:1-11). St. John called this miracle a "sign"—a sign of who Jesus is.

The young bride and groom had run out of wine to serve their guests at the wedding celebration! Perhaps Mary was in some way involved with the wedding preparations, for she knew of the need and simply mentioned it to Jesus: "They have no wine" (John 2:3). At first Jesus didn't seem to want to get involved. He replied, "Woman, what concern is that to you and to me? My hour has not yet come" (2:4). We might interpret his response as something like this: "This is your problem, not mine. Don't get me involved in it, because I'm not ready to perform any signs." Doesn't it sound like an emphatic "no"? But not to Mary. Her faith was so strong, her desire so ardent, that Jesus was moved to respond. Mary's last recorded words in sacred Scripture, addressed to those who waited on the tables at the wedding celebration, were filled with a confident expectation that Jesus would do something: "Do whatever he tells you" (2:5). And Jesus knew this. How could he resist such confident faith? Mary's faith moved Jesus to reveal his glory by working his first miracle of changing water into wine. What was his glory? The majesty and power that he had with the Father. St. John adds that after seeing this miracle, "his disciples believed in him" (2:11).

The disciples' belief in Jesus is a very important effect of our Lord's first miracle because, as St. John stresses, faith in Jesus is the very beginning of eternal life (see John 5:24; 20:31). So we can say that the miracle at Cana produced a life-giving faith in Jesus' first disciples. This faith and life came to them through the intercession of Mary, since it was her unwavering confidence that moved Jesus to work the miracle. In this way, the Cana story reveals the beginning of the faith of the Church community. And since faith leads to life, Mary can again be seen as the mother of life in the Church. This is why Pope Paul VI appropriately gave Mary the beautiful title of "Mother of the Church" in his speech at the end of the third session of the Second Vatican Council in 1964.[3]

Mary's example of faith also inspires us to believe. Her directive "Do whatever [my Son] tells you," which was addressed to the waiters, is just as well addressed to the apostles and to us. It was a woman's responsibility to raise her child in the fundamentals of the faith. Then, when the child came of age, the father and others would teach that child. So in this account of the wedding at Cana, we could say that Mary was handing the disciples over to Jesus. "Do whatever [my Son] tells you." Her work as our mother is to hand us to Jesus, who will teach us the fullness of all we are called to be and to do. She puts us into the care of her son. Not that she stops caring for us—not at all—but she moves us over to the one who will teach us the fullness of our life-giving faith.

Mary Consoles Us

Mary also brings life to us by consoling us in our struggles and sufferings. Despite the fact that Our Lady had no sin whatsoever in her own life, she was given a great share in suffering, which culminated at the foot of the cross. Her sufferings were always connected with the sufferings of her divine Son and were endured for our salvation. The holy man Simeon, at the presentation of the Child Jesus in the Temple, had prophesied this when he said to Mary, "This child is destined for the falling and the rising of many in Israel, and to be a sign that will be opposed . . . and a sword will pierce your own soul too" (Luke 2:34-35). Mary shared deeply in the sufferings of her Son because they were the Father's will for our salvation. When she moved Jesus to work his first miracle at Cana, she actually "hastened him on to his hour"—to the fulfillment of his life's public mission, ultimately to his suffering, death, and resurrection! As Archbishop Fulton Sheen once remarked, "What other mother would have ever sent her own son onto a battlefield?" Only her love for the Father's will and for our salvation could move Mary to do this.

No stranger to suffering in her own lifetime, Our Lady is filled with great compassion to assist us and console us in our own sufferings during our earthly pilgrimage. One of my favorite stories that illustrates this point involves my own patron saint, Andrew the Apostle. When he died and got to heaven, his brother St. Peter was already on the job at the heavenly gate. St. Andrew immediately asked, "Peter, where is she?" St. Peter instinctively knew who his brother was talking about, and he said, "Andrew, she is not up here in heaven. She is down on earth, drying the tears from the eyes of all her suffering children there."

Mary gives us life as she supports us in our struggles and our sufferings, through which—in the paradox of Christian life—we grow closer to Christ. There is no way we can come closer to Jesus without in some way sharing his cross as Mary did.

Mary Prays for Us

Finally, Mary is a mother of life to us because she prays and intercedes for us. The first chapter of the Acts of the Apostles says that Mary was with the apostles after the Ascension, awaiting the coming of the Holy Spirit: "All these [the apostles] were constantly devoting themselves to prayer, together with certain women, including Mary the mother of Jesus, as well as his brothers" (1:14). Since the disciples prayed together for nine days, this time of ardent prayer can be seen as the first novena of the Church. Mary was in the midst of those first members of the Church as they waited and prayed for the promised gift of the Holy Spirit at Pentecost. Since the Holy Spirit is the Spirit of life in us, Mary's role is to help bring us life by interceding for the gift of the Holy Spirit to come to us as he came to those first disciples of Jesus.

Mary Makes Us the Family of Christ

Although we do not often realize this, we respond to Jesus in many ways. In his *Letter to All the Faithful*, St. Francis of Assisi says that we are "the brides, the brothers, and the mothers of our Lord Jesus Christ." Mary as our mother helps us to relate to Jesus in all of these ways.

St. Francis says that a person is a bride of Christ "when his faithful soul is united with Jesus Christ by the Holy Spirit." This means that there is a spiritual spousal relationship between Christ the Divine Bridegroom and the soul. The union with Christ is not physical but it is a union with him by grace and charity. Jesus said, "Abide in my love" (John 15:10). When we live in the state of grace, we remain in Christ's love, much as spouses, in their union, abide or remain in the love of one another.

St. Francis says that we are brothers of Christ "when we do the will of his Father who is in Heaven." Jesus taught this clearly. At the time our Lord was in a house preaching, and his mother and some of his relatives were outside; they couldn't get into the house because it was so crowded. Word reached Jesus: "Your mother and your brothers are standing outside, wanting to speak to you." Jesus looked around and said, "Whoever does the will of my Father in heaven is my brother and sister and mother" (Matthew 12:47-50). Jesus said this because when we are doing the Father's will, we are in a union of friendship and love with him. Elsewhere he had said, "Those who have my commandments and keep them are those who love me" (John 14:21). In this way, we enjoy being children of the Father and brothers and sisters of Christ.

St. Francis also said we are mothers of Christ "when we enthrone him in our hearts and souls by love with a pure and sincere conscience, and give him birth by doing good. This, too, should be an example to others." This means that we are mothers of Christ, first of all, when Christ lives spiritually in us. This happens when we have Christ living in us through grace.

We are also mothers of Christ when we help to bring Christ to life in others. St. Paul himself used maternal imagery to describe his relationship with his own disciples, his converts. He said, "I am again in the pain of childbirth until Christ is formed in you" (Galatians 4:19). If St. Paul could say this of himself, how much more can we say this of Mary and her relationship to us?

We, like St. Paul, have a similar mission to help bring Christ to life in others. How do we do this? First of all, by our good example. Have you ever heard the saying "You may be the only gospel someone will ever read"? People have to see Christ in us. There is a story about a young man who out of curiosity went to see the great St. John Vianney, the Curé of Ars. This young man was an atheist, but by the end of his visit with that holy priest, he was filled with great faith in God. Back home he met a friend, who upon seeing the dramatic change in him, said, "What? How can you be so fervent in faith? You don't even believe that there is a God!" The young man answered, "I know that there is a God. I saw him living in that priest!" So our good example can help others recognize Christ in us, and that can be the first way we can help bring Christ to birth in others.

Second, we bring Christ to life in others by praying for them. By interceding for the grace of conversion for someone—whether it is conversion from no faith or from a life of sin—we are helping to bring him or her to life in Christ.

Finally, we bring Christ to life in others by sharing the word of God with them. If you instruct children in some religious setting or train your own children, you are doing the work of evangelization in a mothering role. Remember that a Jewish mother teaches the basics of the faith to her children. Similarly, we may do this with others who become our children in Christ. St. Padre Pio often spoke of his "spiritual children," whose life in Christ he supported through his offering of the Mass and the sacraments, as well as through his prayers and good example.

Mary Reveals Herself to Us

Mary's role as our spiritual mother might seem to be carried out completely "behind the scenes," but she shows the depth of her concern for her children through her many apparitions. Through these appearances to simple, unassuming adults and even children, Mary has given the Church important messages, called us all to prayer, and affirmed the value and sanctity of life.

Paris, France. In 1830 Our Lady appeared to Catherine Labouré (now St. Catherine), expressing her concern about all of the evils that were occurring in the world and especially in France. St. Catherine then had a vision that was later portrayed on what has come to be called the "Miraculous Medal."

As depicted on the medal, Mary had rays coming down from her hands, actually from gems on her fingers. St. Catherine noticed very bright lights coming from some of the gems, faint lights coming from others, and no lights at all from still other gems.

When St. Catherine asked Mary about the differences, she said the bright rays of light represented the many graces she obtained for her children who asked her for much. The faint rays represented the fewer graces she obtained for those of her children who asked her for only a little. And then, almost with a tinge of sadness, she explained that the gems that gave off no rays of light represented the other graces she wished to obtain for her other children, "but they never asked me."

So Mary is always ready to come to our aid. We just need to ask her.

Fatima, Portugal. Mary showed her motherly love again in 1917 at Fatima, Portugal, when she appeared to three shepherd children, Jacinta and Francisco Marto and Lúcia de Santos. This time Our Lady came to bring a message of grave concern and warning for the peace of the world. She explained that the evil we know as Communism would begin in Russia and that it would provoke wars as well as persecution of the Church. She asked us to pray and offer sacrifices for peace and for the conversion of sinners.

Our Lady's message of prayer, penance, and reparation is absolutely essential to preserve Christian values and bring world peace. Pope John Paul II has said that the message of Fatima is more important and more urgent now than when Our Lady first gave it to us in 1917![4]

Guadalupe, Mexico. Perhaps the message of Mary as the mother of life is nowhere more vivid than in the message and image of Our Lady of Guadalupe. On December 9, 1531, Our Lady appeared to an Aztec peasant named Juan Diego, who is now a canonized saint. At the time of the apparitions, December 9 was the date of the feast of the Immaculate Conception. (It's now December 8.) There were four apparitions to St. Juan Diego and another apparition to his uncle, Juan Bernardino, who was quite ill at the time. Mary appeared to his uncle and healed him.

The image of Our Lady of Guadalupe, miraculously imprinted on St. Juan Diego's cloak, speaks a message about life. First, it shows that Mary is carrying Christ within her. She is wearing a dark cord with two tassels hanging down from her waist, called a *cinta*, which was worn only by pregnant women. And photographs of the image, studied by scientists, reveal a slight protrusion of the abdomen, indicating Our Lady is carrying the Christ Child in her womb.

An interesting symbol of life on the image is a particular four-petaled flower called the "Flower of the Sun," which is placed directly over Mary's womb. To the Aztecs, who worshipped the sun, the appearance of this sun flower heralded the birth of someone great who would inaugurate a new era. Mary's Son would be the Son of life. In fact, Mary described herself to St. Juan Diego as the mother of all the living.

The image of Our Lady of Guadalupe communicated a sense of dignity to each person and of the sanctity of human life. This brought an end to the practice of human sacrifice among the Aztecs. Mary told the people about a God who sacrificed his own body and blood so that all people could live. And within ten years of Mary's appearance, nearly nine million Aztec people embraced the Catholic faith.

Through her appearance as Our Lady of Guadalupe, Mary teaches us respect for the dignity of human life in all its manifestations—for the unborn, for the disabled, for the elderly, and for the terminally ill. That is why we pray to Mary to restore the sacredness of life, especially under her title of Our Lady of Guadalupe.

Mary truly deserves to be called the mother of life. Let us ask for her prayers so that we may help to restore the God-given dignity of every human life that has been degraded by abortion, euthanasia, or assisted suicide. Furthermore, let us ask her prayers so that all may come to the fullness of life that her Son promised when he said, "I came that they may have life, and have it to more abundantly" (John 10:10).

Part Two

OUR TEACHER

LEARNING FROM MARY TO TRUST GOD

A n old Chinese proverb says, "The journey of ten thousand miles begins with the first step." We are all on a long journey of faith, the journey of a lifetime. In some ways, we take another "first step" every day of our lives. St. Peter says that all of us are merely pilgrims and strangers in this world of ours (see 1 Peter 2:11). We're like the cowboy in the old western movies who would come into town and say, "I'm just passing through." We are passing through this earthly life, because our true homeland is heaven.

When Pope John Paul II wrote his encyclical on the Blessed Mother (*Redemptoris mater*), he stressed Mary's pilgrimage of faith. Mary made the same journey that we do. And because she has gone before us, we can learn from her. She can be our guide, our teacher, for our own pilgrimage of faith. One of the most important lessons we can learn from Mary is how to trust God, especially when our faith is being tested and we are not sure where the Lord is leading us.

Let us recall the words of the archangel Gabriel to Our Lady: "Hail, full of grace, the Lord is with you!" (Luke 1:28, RSV). Pope John Paul II pointed out that this was God's gift to Mary—to favor her so highly that he filled her with grace!

And what was Mary's response to God's gift of grace? Her response was to believe and, in her faith, to trustingly commit her whole life to God. The greatness of this response is reflected in the words of her aged cousin Elizabeth at the time of the visitation. As the women greeted each other, Elizabeth said, "Blessed are you among women, and blessed is the fruit of your womb. And why has this happened to me, that the mother of my Lord comes to me? . . . Blessed is she who believed that there would be a fulfillment of what was spoken to her by the Lord" (Luke 1:42-45).

On a pilgrimage to Israel, I had the opportunity to visit the beautiful spot in a town near Jerusalem called Ain Karim, where tradition says that Elizabeth was staying during her pregnancy. There are about a hundred steps to climb up the side of a little hill to reach a gate at the entrance of a courtyard. According to tradition, it was here that Mary and Elizabeth embraced. As I approached this very holy place, I seemed to sense something of the joy that Mary expressed in her Magnificat: "My soul magnifies the Lord, / and my spirit rejoices in God my Savior" (Luke 1:46-47). That was Mary's response—she believed and trusted in great joy.

In his encyclical, Pope John Paul II noted that Mary advanced in her pilgrimage of faith. In this way, Our Lady teaches us that being a Christian is not a static experience; we have to mature in our Christian life. Just as we grow physically and mature emotionally, so we have to develop spiritually, and that is what our pilgrimage of faith and love is all about. It is about learning to trust God as Mary did.

Growing in trust as our response to God's grace takes time. In fact, it takes precisely the span of the lifetime God gives each one of us here on earth. With perhaps the exception of martyrs, who die suddenly with a supreme love that motivates them to lay down their lives for Jesus, no one becomes perfect all at once. I have always liked the bumper sticker that says, "Be patient with me. God isn't finished with me yet." For this reason, we all have to be patient with ourselves as well as with one another.

It is a temptation, a fantasy, to think that there is instant holiness. In our lives today, we are spoiled because we are used to having so many things instantly. We have microwave ovens; we push a few buttons and in a minute or two the food comes out, hot and ready to eat. We send "instant messages" through cyberspace. We even have instant coffee—although it usually isn't as good as the kind that takes longer to brew. We can do so many things quickly. But that doesn't work with holiness on our journey of faith. Holiness is not something you become or do all at once. You grow in it. We need to be transformed into an ever greater likeness of Jesus. As St. John the Baptist expressed it, "[Jesus] must increase, but I must decrease" (John 3:30). We need to keep trying. We need to take the next step, each day trying to do our best.

There is no better companion on our journey of faith than Mary, for she is our model and our teacher, as well as our mother. She gives us the good example we need to follow on our pilgrimage of life.

CHAPTER 3

Mary, Our Model in Faith

During the Second Vatican Council, the bishops voted on whether to have a separate document about Mary or to put a chapter about her at the end of the most important document of Vatican II, which was called *Lumen gentium* or the Dogmatic Constitution on the Church. By one of the narrowest margins of the entire council, the bishops voted to include Mary as part of—at the end of—the document on the Church. When the secular press reported on the vote, they presented it as a "demotion" of Mary because she wasn't given her own special document. At the time, another brother and I were at a friend's home. After hearing the negative news reports about Our Lady, an old Italian woman asked in great distress, "Brothers, are they throwing the Blessed Mother out of the Church?" I answered, "If they do that, I'm afraid they'll have a big problem with her Son!"

Actually, the bishops were trying to show us that Mary is an integral part of the Church. There was a certain wisdom in that decision. The Holy Spirit seemed to have guided that vote because we need to see Mary as vitally linked to the life of the Church—and to our personal lives as well. Then we can imitate her virtues.

One of the greatest of Mary's virtues that we can imitate is her trust. Many people of faith can say without any difficulty that they *believe* in God, but how many can really say that they *trust* him. Mary not only believed in God but she trusted him so completely that she was able to totally surrender her life to his will.

FAITH: BELIEVING *AND* TRUSTING

The Jewish people knew that there are two aspects of faith. One aspect is intellectual: it takes place entirely in our mind. This is the kind of faith we're talking about when we say that we believe someone. To believe someone is to intellectually assent to what they have told us, because we consider them to be a reliable source. The Jewish people knew that the truths revealed to them came from God, who can neither deceive nor be deceived, and so they believed in them. When we say "I believe" as we recite the Creed, we express our intellectual faith and assent to all of its statements, because we know that they have been revealed by God. And when we finish many of our prayers, we express this aspect of faith in them by adding the word "amen" (So be it). So faith focuses us, first of all, on what we believe as truths that God has revealed.

The Jewish people also knew that faith didn't just consist of a purely intellectual assent—it also had to touch the heart. This second aspect of faith is trust. When we trust, we go beyond merely believing in the truth of what we have been told to surrendering ourselves to the one we believe. Because this aspect of faith is active, it enabled the Hebrews to give themselves completely to the service of God.

When we not only believe God intellectually but also trust him with our heart, then we have the kind of faith that enables us to do his will. This is what happens when we commit our lives to God: we put our life on the line, ready to act. To have trust in God means to believe in his word and then to surrender ourselves to him by putting his word into action.

This is the kind of faith that Mary practiced. It is the kind of faith that we too must practice—to trust in almighty God and his work in our lives.

MARY'S YES — CHEERFUL SURRENDER

Our Lady's trust can be seen, first of all, in her response to the message God sent to her through the archangel Gabriel. When he appeared to Mary in Nazareth, he addressed her as "full of grace" (Luke 1:28, RSV), as the highly favored daughter of God. He told her that she would conceive a son. But Mary was still a virgin, and so she needed to have the archangel's message clarified. How could she bear a son if she intended to remain a virgin?

The archangel assured her how this would happen: "The Holy Spirit will come upon you, / and the power of the Most High will overshadow you; / therefore the child to be born will be called holy, / the Son of God" (Luke 1:35, RSV).

Once Mary received this clarification, she didn't hesitate to give her consent. Without delay she quickly responded, "Behold, the handmaid of the Lord. May it be done to me according to your word" (see Luke 1:38). In Our Lady's concise answer, we find the greatest trust.

In saying, first of all, "I am the handmaid of the Lord," Mary was saying, "I am ready to do whatever God asks of me. My whole life is devoted to serving him." Servants and handmaids don't do their own will. They do the will of the one they serve.

Then Mary added, "Let it be done to me according to your word." In Latin this response has traditionally been called Mary's *fiat*—"let it be done." Mother Teresa of Calcutta often used the expression "Mary gave God permission." That is what Mary did. What she said, in effect, was "I am here to serve him; therefore let God do in my life whatever he wishes." Mary completely entrusted herself to almighty God and to his plan for her and for the salvation of the world.

Some years ago, I was in New Mexico, giving a retreat for the Missionaries of Charity. They have a great devotion to the Immaculate Heart of Mary. Every year in preparation for the feast of Mary's Immaculate Heart, the sisters make a three-day retreat, called a *triduum*. It is always based on their community's threefold "spirit": loving trust, total surrender, and cheerfulness. They encapsulate the spirit of Mother Teresa, the order's foundress, who saw these three virtues as characteristic of Our Lady. Mary lovingly trusted the word of the archangel, God's message to her, and then in total surrender she gave her consent. She said yes, and she did it generously and cheerfully.

With Mary as our example, we too must learn to trust almighty God—to cheerfully surrender ourselves to his work in our lives. But trusting in God is one of the hardest lessons on our faith journey to learn and one of the spiritual tasks that takes the longest to accomplish. Why? Because we harbor so many fears.

CHAPTER 4

Fear, the Enemy of Trust

When you were a little child, did you ever need your mom or dad to rescue you from some kind of predicament—for example, climbing too high in a tree? Your dad may have come right away when you called him, and there he stood at the bottom of the tree, ready to save you. All you had to do, he said, was to climb down backwards. He would be with you the whole way, ready to catch you if you slipped. And yet, as much as you believed that what he said was true and as much as you trusted him never to let anything happen to you, maybe you just couldn't do it—you were too paralyzed with fear to move. So until you overcame your fear, you weren't going to get out of that tree.

Fear is the enemy of trust. Our fear prevents us from giving ourselves completely to God. It makes us hesitant; it prompts us to hold back. We might be afraid to put our trust in God because we don't know what lies in store for us. Or perhaps we're only comfortable when we're calling the shots, and we're afraid of giving control of our life completely to God. Then again, fear that we're not good enough might keep us from allowing God to work through us. And then there's the question of what God might ask of us if we do surrender all that we are to him. What if he asks more than we are capable of giving? And finally, what if we invest everything in God and then feel that he has abandoned us? It's fears like these that we will need to overcome with Mary's help if we are ever going to be able to put our trust in our almighty Father as she did.

FEAR OF THE UNKNOWN

One fear that interferes with our ability to trust God concerns the unknown. We don't know what lies beyond our immediate experience, and we are reluctant to go beyond what we know.

Years ago a former teacher of mine wrote me with the news that her mother was close to death. "My mother is very afraid," she said. Trying to be helpful, I wrote a few thoughts about how to trust in God.

She wrote back to me, explaining that I did not need to be concerned. "My mother isn't afraid that she won't be with God after she dies. She's simply afraid of the unknown. She doesn't know what lies beyond."

In the spiritual life—even before we face the grave—there is a certain measure of the unknown. If we want a perfect example, we can turn to Abraham, that man of great faith. What was the first thing God asked of Abraham and his wife, Sarah? He said, "Go from your country and your kindred and your father's house to the land that I will show you" (Genesis 12:1). Did you ever find on the map a country called "the land that I will show you"?

There is no place by that name. Abraham didn't know where he was going. He would know it only when he got there.

As travelers today, we are spoiled. If we are planning a trip, we can contact a travel agent, who will work out all the details for our trip and send us the itinerary. Or we might belong to an automobile association, and they will send us a map with a colored line to show us what route to take and where to stop and what to see along the way. Or we might go to an online service that gives us every detail, every twist and turn. We might even have a navigational system right on the dashboard of our car that tells us where we are and when we need to turn.

With technology, we're generally used to knowing where we are going all the time. Everything is clearly pointed out to us. But when we begin the journey of faith, we don't know what lies ahead. We commit ourselves and entrust ourselves to God to enter into the unknown, and God unfolds our lives ahead of us, one step at a time.

Years ago when a young bride and groom stood at the altar ready to exchange their marriage vows, the priest would read to them from the traditional "Exhortation before Marriage," reminding them about their future. He would tell them that their married life would be filled with joys and sorrows, hopes and disappointments, successes and failures. Since these things are a part of every human life, they were to be expected in their life together. On their wedding day, of course, this is all hidden from their eyes. They simply want to say, "I do." A wise priest I

Following Mary to Jesus

knew many years ago would often say, "Love is blind, but marriage is the eye-opener!" That's why it would not be a surprise if some years later they might wonder, "Did I really say '*I do*'?" Similarly, when a priest approaches the altar to be ordained, he doesn't know what lies ahead. Religious brothers and sisters vowing poverty, chastity, and obedience all the days of their lives are likewise entering into the unknown.

We're all like Abraham and Sarah, embarking on a journey into the unknown. But one thing that Abraham and Sarah did know—and that we must learn from them—is that the God who called them to go forth from their own land would go with them. That's what trust is all about. When we commit ourselves to God, we don't know what the future holds. But we know who holds the future. We know that God will be with us. We must always trust his unseen presence arranging things in our lives by his loving providence.

In our daily spiritual pilgrimage, we learn to trust by reaching out our hands, just as a popular song said years ago: "Put your hand in the hand of the man who stilled the waters. Put your hand in the hand of the man who calmed the sea." It's true! Here's an example of how trust works. A baby in the womb of its mother has no choice in being born. It reaches a certain point in development, and then birth takes place. But let's say that the baby had a choice—to be born or to stay in the womb. He or she might think, "I'm protected here. I'm being fed and taken care of. What more do I need? Why leave this safe place? Look at the security I have. If I'm born, I don't know what is on the other side of my mother's womb. What troubles await me in the outside world?" Now, if a baby chose to stay in that small enclosure, we know what he or she would be missing!

As we face the unknown of eternity, we can take that same attitude: "I want to hold on to what I know and what I have here." But we are promised a much more beautiful world on the other side. St. Paul wrote, "No eye has seen, nor ear heard, / nor the human heart conceived, / what God has prepared for those who love him" (1 Corinthians 2:9). Faith always leads us more and more into the unknown, except in one aspect: we know that God is with us. Never, never forget that fact, because that is where trust begins. We can commit ourselves simply because we know that God is always with us.

Our Lady didn't let any fear of the future or of the unknown keep her from giving her unreserved consent when the archangel Gabriel presented her with God's plan for her life. Without doubt, Mary knew from the Scriptures that the Servant foretold by Isaiah (see Isaiah 53) would have much to suffer. Yet she didn't hesitate to give her total surrender, despite realizing that a significant share in that suffering would fall to her. In fact, when the holy man Simeon, at the presentation of the Child Jesus in the Temple, foretold to Mary that her heart would be pierced by a sword of sorrow (see Luke 2:28-35), she didn't hesitate, didn't back away. Her yes never became a no; it didn't even become a "maybe I have to think about it again." Perhaps Mary, a virgin, would have also realized in the sacred event of the Annunciation that Isaiah had foretold that a "'virgin shall conceive and bear a son, / and they shall name him Emmanuel,' which means, 'God is with us'" (Matthew 1:23; Isaiah 7:14). Mary never faltered in her trust, because she knew that God would always be with her to help her fulfill what he was asking of her.

FEAR OF NOT BEING IN CONTROL

Our trust can also be hindered by the fear of not being in control. Have you ever been a passenger in a car with a driver who made you nervous? Maybe he turned around and had an animated conversation with someone in the backseat. I used to know someone who would take his hands off the steering wheel when he drove. How many Hail Marys I secretly prayed! With drivers like these, you as a passenger are not in control. You feel helpless. You feel like you want to reach over and grab hold of that steering wheel.

There's a story told about a priest and a bus driver who died and arrived at the heavenly gate at the same time. They both knocked and asked St. Peter to be admitted. The saint with the keys to the kingdom replied, "Well, I have to see if you both deserve to come in here." He went off to check the records and returned a few minutes later. He let the bus driver right in, but he told the priest that he had to wait outside.

The priest got very upset. "St. Peter," he said, "I don't begrudge anybody's getting into heaven, but I thought that since I was a

PART TWO | OUR TEACHER: LEARNING FROM MARY TO TRUST GOD

priest on earth, I might at least go in with the bus driver, if not a little ahead of him. Instead, here he goes in ahead of me, and I have to wait outside. I think you owe me an explanation." So St. Peter said, "Father, I will be very honest with you. I checked the records carefully, and this is what I found: When you preached your sermons, they were so boring that you put half the people to sleep. But when this guy was driving the bus, everybody was praying!"

How many circumstances in life seem beyond our control? At times, there are too many to count! In a panic, we may ask, "How can I accept them? How can I live with them?"

Once when giving a retreat for a group of college students, I met a young woman from Korea. She shared a story with us of a harrowing experience that happened in her native country when she was about thirteen years old. She was a passenger on a bus that was speeding along the side of a mountain. The road had sharp curves and no guardrails. Everyone on that bus was panicking, except for one young boy, fast asleep, in the row ahead of her. "Wake up," the girl said to him. "We're going so fast. We're in great danger. Aren't you afraid?" The little boy looked up and said, "No, I'm not afraid. The bus driver is my father." Now that's trust!

There used to be a bus company slogan that said, "Take the bus, and leave the driving to us." God says something similar to us: "Put your life in my hands, and then let me lead you!"

Our Lady experienced situations we could describe as "out of control," or at least out of her immediate control. But instead of panicking, she turned the situations over to God and trusted him to take care of them. For example, when St. Joseph realized that Mary was "with child" and did not know how the child had been conceived, he was considering divorcing her quietly. This had to have been a trial for Mary, as it was for Joseph. She realized his anguish over her pregnancy, yet she did not attempt to "resolve the crisis" on her own. She trusted that God would resolve it for her earthly spouse. She did not give way to fear or panic. Like St. Joseph, who was considering prayerfully what to do in the situation, Our Lady prayed that the Lord might intervene. And he did!

> An angel of the Lord appeared to him in a dream and said, "Joseph, son of David, do not be afraid to take Mary as your wife, for the child conceived in her is from the Holy Spirit. She will bear a Son, and you are to name him Jesus, for he will save his people from their sins." (Matthew 1:20-21)

Another situation that was out of Mary's control was King Herod's attempt to kill the child Jesus. In the face of Herod's cruelty, Our Lady placed herself and the child Jesus under St. Joseph's loving care. She followed the directions given to her spouse by an angel in a dream: "Get up, take the child and his mother, and flee to Egypt" (Matthew 2:13). There was no panic, no fear. Our Lady knew that God was in control, not Herod. The conviction of her trust was that nothing can ever happen unless God either wants it or permits it! That same conviction must be ours.

A third example of a situation seemingly out of control for Mary was the loss of the young Jesus in the temple for three days. This was, no doubt, a source of much sorrow and concern for Mary. She even admitted as much when she addressed Jesus: "Son, why have you done this to us? Did you not know that your father and I would search for you in great sorrow?" (see Luke 2:48). Mary and Joseph were concerned for Jesus' well-being and safety, since he had been specially entrusted to their care. It was their confidence in God's good purposes that allowed Mary and Joseph to continue their search until Jesus was found.

St. Augustine's Commentary

Of course, holy Mary did the will of the Father. And therefore it means more for Mary to have been a disciple of Christ than to have been the mother of Christ. . . .

While the Lord was passing by, performing divine miracles, with the crowds following him, a woman said: *Fortunate is the womb that bore you.* And how did the Lord answer, to show that good fortune is not really to be sought in mere family ties? *Rather blessed are those who hear the word of God and keep it* (Luke 11:27-28). So that is why Mary, too, is blessed, because she heard the word of God and kept it.[5]

When Jesus at times tests our trust in him by seeming to be "lost," let us allow the example of Mary and Joseph to encourage us. The situation may seem to be out of our control, but it is always under God's total control.

FEAR OF BEING UNWORTHY

A third fear that interferes with the faith of many good people is the fear of not being good enough. Many of us grew up with a bundle of insecurities. For example, despite our very best efforts, we may have been criticized for not doing better in our schoolwork or for not excelling in competition with others, especially in sports programs. We may have come from a dysfunctional family. Perhaps we never knew what mood our parents would be in or whether we would find mom or dad warm and loving.

However, we need to remember that we were not raised in the Holy Family. We didn't have Mary and Joseph as our parents. Our parents all had their faults, and many of us have the emotional scars to show for it. Sometimes when our insecurities fester, we think, "If I'm not perfect, God isn't going to love me." Or, "I wonder what I have to do today to make sure that God doesn't get angry with me?"

This kind of thinking is wrong, because God loves us far more than we could ever begin to imagine. God is not waiting to get angry with us. He is not surprised by what we do, by our faults or by our mistakes. When we lose our patience or get distracted in prayer, God doesn't need an aspirin for a headache. He is not upset. His love is all-encompassing.

In his first inaugural address, Franklin D. Roosevelt said, "The only thing we have to fear is fear itself—nameless, unreasoning, unjustified terror which paralyzes needed efforts to convert retreat into advance."[6] This is also true in our relationship with God. We know that fear often paralyzes us and prevents us from acting. It ties us up on the inside, and it doesn't allow us to release our potential for good. To grow in the spiritual life, we have to let go of our fear of not being perfect. Can we trust God enough to claim the truth that God already knows all our faults and yet accepts and loves us for who we are? Knowing that God accepts us can allow us to accept ourselves.

The fear of being unworthy is ultimately overcome by the virtue of humility. St. Francis of Assisi described humility when he said, "What a man is in the sight of God, so much he is, and no more."[7] In other words, if people praise us but God does not, their praise doesn't increase our worth. The reverse is also true: if people condemn us but God does not, their condemnation doesn't decrease our worth. Humility means that I can acknowledge my sins when I have done something wrong. But it also means that I acknowledge that God is the source of my gifts and graces, by recognizing the good things he does in and through me.

Only her divine Son could be said to have had more humility than Our Lady. She expressed her profound humility in the opening verses of her beautiful canticle, the Magnificat:

"My soul magnifies the Lord,
    and my spirit rejoices in God my Savior,

for he has looked with favor on the lowliness of his servant.
Surely, from now on all generations will call me blessed;
for the Mighty One has done great things for me,
and holy is his name." (Luke 1:46-49)

Because Our Lady cooperated fully with every grace God gave her, she had no sins to acknowledge. But she clearly acknowledged God as the source of all her graces and blessings. She called herself God's lowly servant, echoing her words to the archangel Gabriel, "I am the handmaid of the Lord." God the Father confirmed Mary's humility when he exalted her by choosing her to be the mother of his own divine Son. This is always God's way—to put down the proud while he raises up the lowly.

FEAR OF AN OVERLY DEMANDING GOD

A fourth fear that complicates our trust can be expressed like this: "If I try to be good, will God take something that I love away from me? What is God going to ask me to do? What sacrifice might God want me to make?" In his famous poem "The Hound of Heaven," Francis Thompson describes this scenario. In effect, he says, "God, I feared that if I have you, I will have nothing else."

We forget that God gave us everything we have in the first place, whether it is our health, our family, our financial status, or our happiness. They are all gifts from God. Sometimes,

From "The Hound of Heaven," by Francis Thompson

I fled Him, down the nights and down the days;
I fled Him, down the arches of the years;
I fled Him, down the labyrinthine ways
    Of my own mind; and in the mist of tears
I hid from Him, and under running laughter.
        Up vistaed hopes I sped;
        And shot, precipitated,
Adown Titanic glooms of chasmèd fears,
From those strong Feet that followed, followed after.
        But with unhurrying chase,
        And unperturbèd pace,
    Deliberate speed, majestic instancy,
        They beat—and a Voice beat
        More instant than the Feet—
    "All things betray thee, who betrayest Me."

    I pleaded, outlaw-wise,
By many a hearted casement, curtained red,
    Trellised with intertwining charities;
(For, though I knew His love Who followed,
        Yet was I sore adread
Lest, having Him, I must have naught beside.)
But, if one little casement parted wide,
    The gust of His approach would clash it to.
        Fear [knew] not to evade as Love [knew] to pursue. . . . [8]

however, he tests his friends in a big way to see how much they love him. Yet even when he tests us, God ends up giving us more than he would ever take from us. That was certainly the experience of Job.

In the late Middle Ages, there was a very famous anchoress who lived like a hermit in a little house attached to—or anchored to—a parish church. We don't know her real name. The name that has come down to us is Lady Juliana or Julian of Norwich, because she lived on the property of the Church of St. Julian in Norwich, England. Her writings give us great confidence in the midst of our trials. She wrote these encouraging words: "[God] did not say 'You shall not be tempest-tossed, you shall not be work-weary, you shall not be discomforted.' But [God] did say 'You shall not be overcome.'"[9] We should often reflect on these words. God didn't say we weren't going to have any trials or difficulties. They are obvious in the lives of all who love him, because to truly love Jesus demands that we become true lovers of the cross. We might say that Jesus could easily speak to us in the words of a song that was quite popular some years ago: "I beg your pardon; I never promised you a rose garden." At least not here! In life we have to take a little rain along with the sunshine.

What can we learn in the midst of the rainstorms? Let us take an example from one of the experiences of the apostles. It shows that they still had difficulty trusting, even though they had Jesus with them. In this incident, our Lord was crossing the Sea of Galilee with his disciples when a fierce storm suddenly blew in (see Mark 4:35-41). The Sea of Galilee was well-known for such sudden storms. So where was our Lord? The gospel says he was on a big mat or cushion, fast asleep in the back of the boat! The twelve apostles, on the other hand, were hanging on for dear life. They must have been thinking, "This is it—we're going down!" At least four of them—Peter, Andrew, James, and John—were experienced fishermen. Yet even they panicked. Some of the apostles went over to Jesus and woke him up, saying, "Teacher, do you not care that we are perishing?" (4:38). They sounded as if they were actually scolding him: "Don't you have any more concern for us? How can you just sleep there and let us go down with the boat?"

What did our Lord do? He got up and commanded the wind and the waves to be still. Immediately they died down! Then he turned to the apostles and said, "Why are you afraid? Have you still no faith?" (Mark 4:40). Even the apostles had to hear such a rebuke. They had been with our Lord for some time now, during which they had seen many of his miracles. And yet, in that moment of trial and fright, they forgot that he loved them so deeply and that he was watching over them very carefully.

Many times when God tests us, doesn't he seem to reach down his hand to save us at just the right moment? That happened to St. Peter in another gospel story (Matthew 14:22-33). Again the apostles were in a boat one evening on a stormy sea, but this time Jesus was not with them. He had stayed on the shore. During the night, the apostles saw what they thought was a ghost walking on the water. But Jesus reassured them: "Take heart, it is I; do not be afraid." When Peter realized that it was Jesus, he called out, "Lord, if it is you, command me to come to you on the water." The Lord responded with a simple command: "Come." So Peter jumped out of the boat and began to walk on the water (14:27-29).

The Gospel of Matthew says that Peter did fine as long as he focused his attention on Jesus. But then Peter took his eyes off the Lord and instead took notice of the strong wind and high waves, and this filled him with great fear. And as fear overwhelmed him, he began to sink into the water. His faith and his trust were disappearing, and when it seemed that he was nearly lost, he reached out his hand to Jesus. "Lord, save me!" he cried out (Matthew 14:30). The Lord pulled him up, but again he had a gentle rebuke: "You of little faith, why did you doubt?" (14:31). It was as if Jesus was saying to Peter, "You were doing so well! Why did you take your eyes off me, Peter? Why did you allow the wind and the waves to cause you to panic?" He got the message!

I'm sure that St. Peter learned from this experience. He grew in the faith that strengthened him in the years ahead. As we face the storms of life, whether they be worries or difficulties within our family or fears that come from struggles in the world around us, let us remember that the Lord is right there. We must not take our eyes off him. He would say to us, "Do you think that I would let you perish?" He is a God who is always faithful.

Fear of the "Dark Night"

Human experience shows us that all of us have an instinctive fear of darkness. Not being able to see allows our imagination to conjure up the presence of all kinds of things that could threaten us in the darkness around us. It is a fear that we generally overcome as we mature. Sometimes people deliberately do things to conquer a fear of the dark. For example, some tribes of Native Americans trained their young boys to become warriors by leaving them alone in a forest overnight. The youths approaching young adulthood would have to conquer their fear of the dark by that experience of being alone. Even St. Francis de Sales deliberately went out into the woods overnight on many occasions to overcome his fear of the darkness. He believed that conquering this particular fear would give him a greater freedom and confidence in the face of life's trials.

If the challenge of conquering our fear of physical darkness is great, even more so is the challenge of conquering our fear of spiritual darkness, which St. John of the Cross called the "dark night of the soul." It is a feeling that many people of great faith have experienced on their journey to the fullness of their life in Christ.

In the first period of spiritual darkness, which St. John of the Cross calls the "dark night of the senses," we experience a sense of the loss of God. It is usually characterized by a notable period of dryness in prayer and an inability to meditate. God seems to have left us. I like to compare this period of dryness to the experience of Our Lady and St. Joseph when they had lost the Child Jesus in the Temple for three days. When we go through this dark night, we also experience the sense of God's silence and his temporary disappearance from our life as a source of great sorrow. Let us remember that Mary and Joseph did not give up searching until they found Jesus. We, in turn, must not give up praying and serving him faithfully until we "find him again" when the period of darkness ends. We will see Christ then in an even more brilliant light.

St. John of the Cross talks about a second kind of spiritual darkness, which he calls the "dark night of the spirit." This generally happens in the lives of people who attain a significant degree of holiness. For example, St. Thérèse of Lisieux experienced an intense spiritual darkness that lasted for almost a year and a half before her death. Such an experience of darkness caused her to have temptations to doubt the very existence of heaven. She offered this great trial in reparation for the sins of atheists. Closer to our own time, Mother Teresa of Calcutta experienced a profound darkness in her soul for about fifty years. It caused her great anguish, because she was tempted to doubt whether God still loved her. Despite it all, through this darkness, Mother Teresa persevered. Even St. Padre Pio would pray in thanksgiving after Mass, "I fear the darkness, the temptations, the dryness, the cross, the sorrows. / Oh, how I need You, my Jesus, in this night of exile! / Stay with me, Jesus, in life with all its dangers. I need you."[10]

The dark night of the spirit is much like the experience of Our Lady at the foot of the cross. During this dark night, God allows the individuals to experience trials that leave them feeling as if they had been crucified with Christ. Misunderstandings, conflicts of all sorts, and often sickness and various forms of interior and exterior sufferings are experienced by someone in this stage, as Mary experienced them on Calvary.

But even as she held the body of her Son at the foot of the cross, Mary never gave up trust in the Father's plan for our salvation. Scripture shows us that she alone, of all the disciples of Jesus, kept alive the hope of the resurrection, based on Jesus' three predictions, not only of his suffering and death but also of his rising from the dead. St. John, the beloved disciple, did not believe that Jesus had risen until he had seen the empty tomb (see John 20:8). St. Mary Magdalene, who was the most faithful of all the women disciples after Our Lady, went to the tomb Easter morning, expecting to anoint a dead body (see Mark 16:1). Mary did not have to see the empty tomb nor did she attempt to anoint the dead body of her Son. She simply trusted his word. Incidentally, this is why the Church has dedicated every Saturday in a special way to the Blessed Mother, because she kept alive the faith of the Church in the resurrection of Jesus from Good Friday until Easter Sunday.

We must learn from Our Lady, then, to trust in the power of Jesus' resurrection and its effect in our own lives. As Archbishop Fulton Sheen used to say, "There cannot be an Easter Sunday without a Good Friday." The dark night will always give way to a glorious day. Perhaps we can find great comfort in a little poem called "Trust Him":

Trust him when dark doubts assail you;
Trust him when your strength is small;
Trust him when to simply trust him
Seems the hardest thing of all!

Trust him—he is ever faithful;
Trust him for his will is best;
Trust him for the heart of Jesus
Is the only place of rest!

Trust him then through doubts and sunshine;
All your cares upon him cast,
Till the storm of life is over,
And the trusting days are past!
(Author unknown)[11]

We need only recall the beautiful Psalm 23: "The LORD is my shepherd, I shall not want. . . . / Even though I walk through the darkest valley, / I fear no evil; / for you are with me; / your rod and your staff— / they comfort me." The Good Shepherd is always with us. We need never be afraid.

CHAPTER 5

Two Convictions That Strengthen Trust

Try as we might, like the child stuck in the tree, we might feel that we still have lingering fears. In that case, there are two convictions or heartfelt beliefs we need to embrace to strengthen our trust: (1) we must believe that God is always with us, and (2) we must believe that through God's providence, all things will work out for our good. Mary encourages us in these convictions every day.

God Is Always with Us

God is always with us at every moment and in every place! And if this is so, then nothing—*nothing*—can ever really harm us. Each day we should pray, "Let me remember, Lord, that nothing will happen to me today that you and I together can't handle." A retreat director many years ago said something that I have never forgotten: "No matter who is against you, if God is with you, then you and God are always in the majority." No matter what we face, since the Lord is always with us, there is no difficulty greater than he is, no obstacle that his power and wisdom can't deal with. We simply need to trust him.

To believe this, we need to be convinced of two further truths in our minds and hearts: (1) without Jesus I can do nothing, and (2) with Jesus I can do anything (see Philippians 4:13). His help and his strength can accomplish what I can't accomplish by my own efforts. "I give them eternal life, and they shall never perish, and no one shall snatch them out of my hand" (John 10:28, RSV). So if he's got you and me in his hands, why should we be afraid? Knowing that God is with us gives us the faith that even "moves mountains" (see Mark 11:22-23). It gives us the trust to take the next step on our journey with him.

> ### St. Teresa's Bookmark
>
> Let nothing trouble you, let nothing frighten you.
> All things are passing; God never changes.
> Patience obtains all things.
> He who possesses God lacks nothing: God alone suffices.

St. Teresa of Ávila used to keep a special bookmark in her prayer book so that it was always at hand when she needed it. Among other things, it said, "Let nothing trouble you. Let nothing frighten you—all things are passing." When we are going through trials in the midst of the storms of life, a very important thing to remember is that these present storms will pass just as all the previous ones did. The bookmark continues, "God never changes." The trials and the moods of life, the ups and downs, come and go, but God always remains the same.

After the Second World War in Europe, investigators discovered certain words inscribed on the wall of a basement where Jewish people had hidden from the Nazis. "I believe in the sun even when it is not shining, I believe in love even when it is not apparent, and I believe in God even when he is silent." This strong expression of belief came from people who went through grave trials, but they had learned to have great confidence in God's presence with them, no matter what their circumstances were.

God Works All Things Together for Our Good

The second conviction that gives us strength to trust God in all things actually follows from the first. Because God is always with us, he will direct all things to work out for the best. St. Paul teaches this clearly. "We know that all things work together for good for those who love God, who are called according to his purpose" (Romans 8:28).

When I look back at my own life experiences, I see how true this has been for me. I was recently reminiscing with a friar I've known for many years. He reminded me of when he and I had lived in a beautiful setting, working in a rewarding ministry. It was a time of many blessings. But then I received word of a transfer. I wasn't looking forward to the change, but I knew it was the will of God. I moved, and the new assignment turned out to

St. Augustine on the "Happy Fault"

Unless Adam had fallen in the body, Christ would not have raised us up to this new life in the spirit. O great and wondrous mystery! . . . The immortal One builds up mortal man, and mortality gives birth to immortality. . . . All this is the result of Eve's action which is remedied through Mary. Happy Eve therefore, through whom death arose; happier still Mary the instrument of purification. Happy Eve as the mother of people; happier Mary, the Mother of our Lord. . . . Eve is the mother of the human race; Mary is the mother of the author of their salvation.

be for the most part a very joyful experience for me. Ironically, I later heard about changes in my former assignment that led me to believe that I would have been very unhappy if I had remained there. Talking with this friar about "old times" showed me how God had been working, even in my disappointments. God knew what he was doing.

God will either prevent difficulties from coming our way by shielding us from them, or he will turn them into some good that will help us grow. That's how St. Augustine looked at original sin. He reasoned that because of sin, God sent us a Redeemer, who brought us an abundance of graces and blessings we would not have had otherwise! This idea is known in Latin as the *felix culpa* or "happy fault." The term is even used in the Exsultet sung at the Easter Vigil: "O happy fault that merited so great a Redeemer."

A big part of our problem with trusting God is that we tend to think that God is going to act "logically"—that is, according to the way we think he should. But God knows better! There is a story about a philosopher who went into a garden one day. He was standing under a giant oak tree that was filled with little acorns. Off to the side of the garden was a fence covered by a vine that had big squashes hanging down from it. The philosopher looked at the contrast between the fragile vine bearing its heavy squashes and the mighty oak tree with its tiny acorns. This led him to think, "You know, if I were God and had created the world, I would have made things just the opposite. I would have put these small acorns on that fragile vine, and I would have taken the heavy squashes and put them on this mighty oak tree." Just then, an acorn fell and hit him right on the head! He had an immediate change of mind: "Thank God I didn't create the world!" God certainly knew what he was doing.

The prophet Isaiah said that God's ways are not our ways (see 55:9). We always figure that God is going to use straight-line logic to deal with our problems. We often think that if something has to happen, God will just do it. But he doesn't always do the things we expect. For example, if we want to cross a street, we figure that we can simply step off the curb and walk straight across. But God, on his part, might put up a detour sign or direct us all around the block to get us to the other side, and we may feel confused, disappointed, or burdened. Yet through it all, he gets us where we have to go. God knows what he is doing.

Cardinal John Henry Newman, in a popular quote from his writings, sums up much of what I have been saying about trust:

> God has created me to do him some definite service; he has committed some work to me which he has not committed to another. I have my mission—I may never know it in this life, but I shall be told it in the next. I am a link in the chain. A bond of connection between persons. He has not created me for naught.
>
> I shall do good, I shall do His work. I shall be an angel of peace, a preacher of truth in my own place while not intending it if I do but keep His commandments. Therefore I will trust him. Whatever I am, I can never be thrown away. If I am in sickness, my sickness may serve him; in perplexity, my perplexity may serve him. If I am in sorrow, my sorrow may serve him. He does nothing in vain [uselessly]. He knows what he is about. He may take away my friends. He may throw me among strangers. He may make me feel desolate, make my spirits sink, hide my future from me—still he knows what he is about.[12]

Trust is only possible for someone who believes in the providence of God. This means believing that today God is already taking care of tomorrow. A Dominican priest, Fr. Henri Lacordaire (d. 1861), said, "All that I know of tomorrow is that God's providence will rise before the sun." He has already provided for tomorrow before the day begins. Trust him. Walk every day with him, and then the trials won't seem so overwhelming while the joys will multiply immensely.

Many of the joys that will come from trusting God won't be apparent immediately, but one always will: a feeling of peace. This is because in God's hands and in the light of eternity, all things work together for good. We are at peace when our minds are not running in worry and anxiety. We talk about "running in place." There is a corresponding mind-set of "running in worry"—about the past or the future. These are always two things we worry a lot about, two things we can't control, because the past is gone and the future is not yet here. If we want peace in our lives, we must trust God and let him take care of the past and the future. As St. Padre Pio would say, "God, my past to your mercy; my future to your providence; my present to your love."

> Take away this star of the sun which illuminates the world: where does the day go? Take away Mary, this star of the sea, of the great and boundless sea: what is left but a vast obscurity and the shadow of death and deepest darkness?
>
> —St. Bernard,
> *In Nativitate B. Mariae Sermo*

Let us ask Mary to be our model and our teacher. It was she who gave us that beautiful example of trust when she acknowledged herself as the handmaid of the Lord: "Let it be done to me according to your word" (Luke 1:38). She entrusted her life to God's plan for her, and she never took back that unqualified *fiat*, that yes she had given to God. Obviously she was gifted beyond all of us, but we can learn little by little, day by day, how to imitate the great trust of Mary.

Our Lady's formula for trust and peace will always remain the same. It is found in her last recorded words in the gospel: "Do whatever he [my Son] tells you" (see John 2:5.) Let us pray to her to fill us with great confidence so that we will never forget that Jesus is always with us. Then we will have nothing to fear.

Part Three

OUR ADVOCATE

MARY PREPARES OUR HEARTS
FOR GOD'S MERCY

In the plan of God, Mary always sets the stage for Jesus, her Son. She always comes before he arrives. In his beautiful encyclical about Mary, Pope John Paul II compared Our Lady to the morning star that appears in the sky before the break of day, and Jesus to the sun that rises in fullness (*Redemptoris mater*, 3). Mary is the dawn; Christ is the fullness of the day.

Mary's coming prepares us in many ways to receive the full blessings that Christ, her Son, will give us. In some ways, she fulfills a role similar to that of St. John the Baptist. When people asked him who he was and what his mission was, he said he was the voice crying out in the wilderness that Isaiah had prophesied about, the one who was to prepare the way of the Lord (see Isaiah 40:3; John 1:23). In her role as our intercessor and advocate, Mary, our Mother of Mercy, shows us her compassionate love and prepares our hearts to receive the mercy of God.

CHAPTER 6

God Desires to Show Us Mercy

Sometimes we can forget that God wants to give us his mercy. As a result, we are tempted to turn away from God when in fact we need him the most. Jesus himself gave us the special gift of the Divine Mercy devotion to show us how much he wants to give us his mercy—and to show us what we need to do to receive it. The Blessed Mother helps us to see that God's mercy is something we all need now.

MERCY: GOD'S MOST ENDEARING AND ENDURING QUALITY

If there is anything God wants us to know about himself, it is that he is always merciful. In fact, in his revelations to St. Faustina, Jesus referred to himself as Divine Mercy. Psalm 136 is the great Jewish litany of thanksgiving and praise for God's mercy. Twenty-six times the refrain echoes, "For his mercy endures forever" (RSV). The Hebrew word translated as "mercy" in the psalm is *hesed*. It means God's enduring love, his faithful loving kindness, especially toward people in distress. The mercy of God moves his heart to be compassionate to us. And this *hesed* of God endures forever!

In one of the prefaces used at Mass, we read these beautiful words: "In love God created man, in justice he condemned him, but in mercy he redeemed him." In other words, it was purely out of his love that God created you, me, and the whole universe. When we sinned—through our first parents as well as through our own personal sins—God, in his justice, had to condemn us. But it was his mercy that redeemed us: God the Father's compassion and mercy moved him to send his divine Son into the world to save us (see John 3:16-17).

We are like the prodigal son that Jesus spoke of in one of his parables. Each of us has gone astray. Our heavenly Father waits—like the father in Jesus' parable—for his child to come home. We get the impression that the father in the parable looked far down that road every day, hoping against hope that his son would return. St. Luke's gospel tells us that he saw his son "while he was still far off." Moved with compassion at the sight of his son, the father "ran and put his arms around him and kissed him" (Luke 15:20).

The Scripture passages that refer to God's mercy were written thousands of years ago for people in a different time and place. But the experience of the Church throughout its long history, even to this day, shows us that God still treats us with mercy, compassion, and patience. We are always in need of his mercy, and today more than ever.

We Need God's Mercy Now

God's mercy holds the answer to all the problems that we face today, whether they be overwhelming world crises such as war, terrorism, and epidemics, or more localized problems such as dissension within and among families or immoral behavior or personal stresses. When confronted with trials and troubles, where are we going to turn but to the mercy of God?

God is always ready to help. We always need to keep this fact in mind. It is especially important in regard to the serious problems that confront the Church daily in our present time. It is extremely distressing to see how many of our Catholic people have lost their faith in God, especially when they hear of problems in the Church. I often think of Jesus' words in the gospel when he said that in the end times, because evil will have spread so far and wide, "the love of many will grow cold" (Matthew 24:12). In saying this, Jesus seemed to be actually answering one of his own questions: "When the Son of Man comes, will he find faith on earth?" (Luke 18:8).

To enkindle that faith once again, we need the mercy of God. We can easily see how divided the Church is today, with so many Catholics abandoning its true teachings, no longer being loyal to the Holy Father, showing disobedience and disrespect for the authority that Christ has given to his Church. Furthermore, there is also the problem of the lack of vocations to the priesthood and religious life. How are all these needs going to be met except by turning once again to the mercy of God?

So when should we invoke God's mercy? The answer is *today*. Scripture says, "Let us therefore approach the throne of grace with boldness, so that we may receive mercy and find grace to help" in due time (Hebrews 4:16). No matter what our age or circumstance, *now* is the time to seek the mercy of God. When does God pour forth his abundant blessings? *Now*, while we are on earth. It is while we are on earth that these graces are given to us. Jesus says, "Store up for yourselves treasures in heaven" (Matthew 6:20). When should we do these things? Our answer again should be right now. When we die, we will meet the Lord in judgment, and at that time he will deal with us with his justice. As he himself said, at his second coming he will repay everyone as their deeds deserve (see Revelation 22:12). But it is now, while we are still on earth, that we can receive the mercy of God, so that later in heaven we can enjoy for all eternity the greatest blessings of the Lord.

THE DEVOTION OF THE DIVINE MERCY

Jesus wants us to receive his mercy, so much so that he gave us one of the greatest blessings in the Church—the devotion of the Divine Mercy. Many Catholics today are familiar with this devotion. It was revealed by our Lord in 1931 when he appeared to a young sister in Poland, St. Faustina Kowalska, and stressed his great love and mercy for all mankind.

Jesus appeared to St. Faustina with red and pale rays emanating from his heart. The rays represent the blood and water that flowed from his pierced side while he hung on the cross. They speak of the love that Jesus showed for you and me. He loved us enough to become human. As St. John said, Jesus was the Word that became flesh (see John 1:14). That very act was an act of infinite mercy.

All through his life Jesus did his Father's will, eventually suffering and dying on the cross in order to win our salvation. So the image of the Divine Mercy represents Jesus' ultimate love for us.

But there's more. Jesus told St. Faustina to reproduce the image that she saw and, at the bottom of it, to put these words: "Jesus, I trust in you." This prayer is meant to be a response—our response—to the mercy of God. Think of it as God's entering into what we might call a contract, or what the Jewish people called a covenant. God made a deal with us. He pledged his love, and then he gave his love for us by dying on the cross. Now he seeks our love in return. How can we express our response to God's mercy? By telling him, "Jesus, I trust in you."

On the bottom of some holy cards with the image of the Divine Mercy, there is an empty space so that each individual can personally fill in the words "Jesus, I trust in you." For many people, this is a concrete act of entrusting themselves to the mercy of God. This is our special personal response.

The Lord has extended his mercy to you and to me by his life, death, and resurrection. He has loved us first. Now we must return that love to him by observing his commandments and doing the things that please him. This is why Jesus said, "If you love me, you will keep my commandments. . . . Those who love me will keep my word, and my Father will love them, and we will come to them and make our home with them" (John 14:15, 23). Jesus himself kept his Father's commandments throughout his whole life. In fact, he was able to say, "I always do what is pleasing to him" (John 8:29).

If we want to receive the mercy of God, we have to pray for it as if it all depends on God. That's what the saints tell us. But we also have to do our part and work as if it all depends on us. God offers us his mercy, but we have a free will and must respond to that grace. We must respond to the mercy Christ has shown us by renouncing our own wills and following the will of God in our lives. How can we do this? This is where the Blessed Mother comes in.

Fr. George Kosicki, CSB, who has devoted his life to spreading the message of Divine Mercy, says that there are three steps in seeking God's mercy. He calls them the ABC's of Mercy: A = *Ask* for mercy; B = *Be* merciful to others; C = *Completely* trust in Jesus. At every step along the way, Mary is our advocate, ready to help us receive the mercy that her divine Son longs to give us.

CHAPTER 7

Mary Helps Us Ask for God's Mercy

When we say the Hail Mary, do we ever stop to think about what we're asking when we pray, "Holy Mary, Mother of God, pray for us sinners now and at the hour of our death"? In the Litany of Our Lady, Mary is called the "refuge of sinners." We never need to be afraid that Mary will turn away from us, even though we may have failed to live as her Son would want us to, even though we may have grievously offended him. We never need to be afraid because Mary is present to us as a mother, welcoming and embracing her repentant children. In fact, Our Lady is constantly interceding for us. That is why we humbly but confidently petition her, "Pray for us sinners!"

Recently I heard a contemporary song that had been made from the words of the Hail Mary—most of them, that is. I noticed that the line "Holy Mary, Mother of God, pray for us sinners" had been changed. Instead it said, "Pray for us, your sons and daughters." This startled me. I thought to myself, "Something is missing."

When I heard this version of the Hail Mary, I said, "They have taken out something very beautiful and very meaningful." You see, if I can go to Mary in my brokenness and sinfulness and know that I am still loved, this helps me view Mary as someone who is compassionate, someone who is always ready to obtain God's mercy for me and draw me most deeply into the mercy of her Son.

Recognizing Our Sinfulness

This is very important. If we lose a sense of our sinfulness, then we minimize the redemption of Jesus. If I have no sins, then why do I need Jesus as a redeemer? If I could save myself—or if I am already perfect—then I have no need of the mercy of Jesus or the compassionate love of the Virgin Mary. But because I know that I need to be forgiven, I can approach the Lord and seek his mercy, assisted by the compassion of his mother.

Think of Jesus' parable of the two men who went into the temple to pray: the publican—a despised tax collector—and the Pharisee (see Luke 18:9-14). The Pharisee simply praised himself. "God, I thank you that I am not like other people: thieves, rogues, adulterers, or even like this tax collector" (18:11). He went through a whole litany of all the seemingly great things he was doing, but unfortunately it was nothing but a litany in praise of himself: I fast twice a week, I pay tithes. In contrast, the publican, with eyes cast down, struck his breast and prayed, "God, be merciful to me, a sinner" (18:13). At the end of the parable, Jesus says that the publican was the one who went home at peace. He asked for mercy, and he received it. The Pharisee would have received mercy, but unfortunately he never asked for it, because he never acknowledged that he needed it.

Like the publican, we too must ask God to grant us mercy for our sins. We don't have to be great sinners to ask for and receive God's merciful forgiveness. When we read about the lives of the saints, like the young St. Augustine, we often see dramatic conversions and a turning away from great sins. Yet even if our sins are small by comparison, if we want to love the Lord more deeply, we need his mercy and his forgiveness every day. Maybe we have neglected some of our duties—our responsibilities to our families or to our neighbors. Maybe we have to ask God to forgive us when we don't serve him with faithfulness or when we get lukewarm or perhaps indifferent from time to time. Furthermore, we need the prayers of Our Lady to keep us close to Christ, her Son. So we invoke Mary as Our Lady of Mercy, because she intercedes for us to receive the forgiveness we need each day. Therefore, all through our life, we will need God's forgiveness and Mary's intercession as well, since as the Council of Trent taught, without an extraordinary grace of God, no one can be free of all sin.

We can be sure that if someone had asked St. Francis of Assisi if he were free of sin, he would have said, "Absolutely not!" At one time, he actually said that he was the world's worst sinner, because he recognized the great graces God had given him but felt that if God had given the same graces to someone else, even a thief, that other person would have been far more grateful and would have used the graces far better than he had.

THE NEED FOR CONVERSION

Today we must implore God to restore a deep appreciation for confession among our Catholic people! Why do so many people today seem to resist going to confession? Many seem to have lost the sense of sin. Maybe the values of society are so changed that people think, "Well, God must have changed his commandments." But he hasn't. Even the saints went to confession. A priest once told me that he was in Rome, vesting for Mass one morning, when he felt a tap on the back of his shoulder. He turned around, and there stood Mother Teresa of Calcutta. "Father, I would like to go to confession," she said. He was thinking to himself, "I should be going to confession to her, not her to me." Padre Pio, who used to hear hundreds of confessions every day, went to confession quite frequently himself. It was said that Pope John Paul II went to confession daily or at least several times each week. The closer you get to God, the more you realize that you need—that you're completely dependent on—his mercy.

After all, what are saints? My favorite definition is that "the saints were simply sinners who kept trying"—they were persevering despite their weaknesses and sins! I like that idea because it encourages me. Because of human weakness, I know I'm never going to be perfect in this life. So many people get all caught up in the need to be absolutely perfect. In heaven we will be perfect, but on earth we will always struggle with human weakness. We will always need God's grace as well as his mercy and forgiveness. But knowing that I can become a saint by being a sinner who keeps trying to be holy encourages me to try every day. It encourages me to claim God's mercy which endures forever, and to be grateful for it. Furthermore, God's mercy is greater than any sin or any evil I could ever do.

It's important to remember that conversion is not usually something that happens all at once. I like the story of a young woman who had experienced a conversion. She was eagerly explaining it to a friend who had asked, "Were you a sinner before your conversion?"

She said, "Oh yes, I was a sinner."

He said, "Well, you aren't a sinner anymore, are you?"

She said, "Oh, I'm still a sinner."

"Well, then what kind of conversion did you have, if you were a sinner before your conversion and a sinner after? What kind of conversion is that?"

She said simply, "Before my conversion I was a sinner running toward sin, and now I'm a sinner running away from it."

When we sinners run away from sin, as our conversion continues day after day throughout our whole lives, we can run into the arms of Our Lady. I am saddened every time I run into people who have done wrong and think they are beyond God's mercy. It is the devil himself who tempts them to despair of God's mercy by telling them, "God won't forgive you for that." Of course God will. The Lord died on the cross for all of us. He will forgive anything, as long as we contritely ask him.

OVERCOMING OUR ATTACHMENT TO SIN

Unfortunately, many people are very attached to sin. For example, even St. Augustine, when he first felt convicted of sin for leading a playboy's life, prayed, "God, give me chastity, but not yet." For years he wasn't ready to give up his sins. He knew that he had to give them up. He also knew that he couldn't do it without God's grace, but he wasn't ready. At least he was honest. Later, however, he lamented that he had wasted all those years of his life.

Perhaps other people resist going to confession because they feel embarrassed. It can be hard to acknowledge our sins, but imagine the peace that comes from receiving that forgiveness.

Then there are people who try to live in denial of their sins, who go through all kinds of rationalizations to excuse themselves. As a result, they carry heavy burdens of denied guilt within themselves. How much better off they would be if they could only face their sins, honestly admit them, and then ask God to forgive them. Then their sins would be taken away. A priest sees this over and over again in the confessional, particularly with sins like abortion. People can't erase them from their memories. They try to push them into the subconscious, but the sin keeps bothering their consciences. I remember one time when I tried to talk a woman out of an abortion. She had already had two; this would have been a third. I said, "Don't you know this is wrong, and it offends God?" Her answer startled me. She said, "Oh, I know it is wrong. I hear babies crying in my dreams."

When people live in denial, their guilt is repressed. The moment they acknowledge the truth, guilt overwhelms them, but that is the moment of mercy. That's the moment when anyone can acknowledge his or her sin before God and seek God's forgiveness, because they have finally acknowledged that sin to themselves. Again, Mary, Our Lady of Mercy, is there at that moment to bring us the forgiveness of her Son.

One of the greatest acts of mercy ever seen in the history of the world happened on Mount Calvary on Good Friday when a thief we know as Dismas turned to Jesus and said, "Jesus, remember me when you come into your kingdom" (Luke 23:42). Despite such a short act of contrition, Dismas showed great humility in acknowledging his sins and, at the same time, a great faith and deep trust in the mercy of Jesus. In response, this good thief heard those beautiful words: "Today you will be with me in Paradise" (23:43). I don't think there are any more consoling words found in the whole Bible than these words of Jesus! Wouldn't you like to hear that? Maybe not right away, but when my day comes, I would love to hear those same words spoken to me.

The mercy of Christ will be there as long as we live, if only we turn to him as St. Dismas did. Imagine how many times during our lifetime we ask Our Lady to intercede for us when we pray these beautiful words: "Holy Mary, Mother of God, pray for us sinners now and at the hour of our death." These words refer to the two most important moments in our whole lives, namely, right *now,* because it is the only moment we actually have, and at the *hour of our death,* because all of our eternity will depend on that moment. That last moment is our final stepping stone into eternity. If we keep asking Mary every day of our lives to remember us now and at that moment of crossing into the next life, then when that moment comes, she will not forget us. She will be there. The Mother of Mercy will be there to bring us before the throne of her Son.

CHAPTER 8

Mary, Who Is Merciful,
Helps Us Be Merciful

Not only must we ask God for mercy, but we, in turn, must be merciful to others. There was a rather famous story that circulated years ago about a big sign at the entrance of the property of a motherhouse of sisters. The sign read, "Private Property. Absolutely no trespassing. Violators will be prosecuted to the fullest extent of the law." And it was signed "The Sisters of Mercy"! Sometimes we contradict ourselves in ways that can appear quite obvious to others.

In all seriousness, how can we as individuals be merciful? To be merciful to someone, we must be able to feel compassion for them. Compassion comes from two Latin words: *passi,* which means "to suffer, to endure," and *com,* which means "with." Compassion means to endure with, to feel what another person is experiencing, especially that person's pain, sorrow, or need. Mary is able to be such a perfect advocate for us because she feels compassion for our daily needs. The perfect mother, she can sense the needs of her children. And she gives us an example that we can follow to show mercy to others.

Mary Responds with Compassion to Our Needs

Our Lady showed compassion in her life and teaches us to do the same. She went to assist her aged cousin, Elizabeth, who was already in her sixth month of pregnancy, because she knew that Elizabeth would need help. She didn't hesitate. Rather, she went "in haste" (Luke 1:39, NAB) and remained for three months, which indicates the depth of her compassionate love.

Mary showed compassion again at the wedding feast of Cana, when she noticed the need of the young bride and groom and then turned to her Son and said, "They have no more wine" (see John 2:3). These words may have sounded like a simple statement of fact, but they were really a special request. Maybe, as a good mother, she was just concerned about the needs of that young couple. I don't think they went to Mary and said, "Look, can you do something about this problem?" They didn't know the power of her Son, but she did. I'm not sure they even knew that they had a problem. In ancient times, wedding feasts went on for about a week, with family and friends dancing and singing and eating and drinking. They were having a good time. So it was more likely Mary who noticed their need. And when she saw that need, what did she do? She simply presented it with great confidence to Jesus: "They have no more wine."

Our Lady's incredible compassion makes her especially concerned for the needs of people who are poor, distressed, or suffering. Our Lady wants everyone to know that she understands their needs and that they can bring their troubles to her. This was the beautiful message of Our Lady of Guadalupe when she appeared to St. Juan Diego, the Indian who was to take her message to Bishop Zumaraga, the bishop of Mexico City. Mary told him that she wanted a shrine built in her honor. "I want a place where my people can come and tell me their needs and their concerns," she said to Juan Diego. "I am truly your merciful mother; yours and all the people . . . who love me, those who seek me, those who trust in me."[13] The poor especially have responded to the beautiful compassion of Mary at Guadalupe, coming to her and asking for her help.

If Mary is compassionate to the poor, she is even more compassionate to those who suffer. Remember: Our Lady of Mercy is also Our Lady of Sorrows. The sword of sorrow pierced her heart, not once, but seven times. It began with the message given to her by an old man named Simeon, when she and Joseph brought the infant Jesus to the Temple to be presented before the Lord. Simeon blessed the Holy Family and then said to Mary, "A sword will pierce your own soul too" (Luke 2:35). In that prophetic message, Mary received the first piercing.

The second sorrow was when the cruel King Herod tried to kill her infant Son. With Joseph, Mary had to flee with the Christ Child to save his life. She was in exile in Egypt, displaced from her land as a refugee, like so many today who are forced to flee their homes due to war or persecution. This particular sorrow came to her because the world would not receive her Son.

Pope John Paul II and the Mystery of Mercy

Mary, then, is the one who has the deepest knowledge of the mystery of God's mercy. She knows its price, she knows how great it is. In this sense, we call her the Mother of mercy: Our Lady of mercy, or Mother of divine mercy. . . .

This revelation [of merciful love] . . . is especially fruitful because in the Mother of God it is based upon the unique tact of her maternal heart, on her particular sensitivity, on her particular fitness to reach all those who most easily accept the merciful love of a mother. This is one of the great life-giving mysteries of Christianity, a mystery intimately connected with the mystery of the Incarnation.

—*Dives in misericordia*, 9

Mary experienced another sorrow when she lost the twelve-year-old Jesus in Jerusalem for three days. Remember what she said to Jesus when she and Joseph found him in the Temple? "Son, why have you treated us like this? Did you not know that your father and I would be searching for you in great sorrow?" (see Luke 2:48). No doubt Mary's sorrow during those three days foreshadowed her sorrow when Jesus would die the terrible death of the cross and be entombed for three days.

Mary experienced the last four of her seven sorrows on Good Friday. The fourth sorrow occurred when she met Jesus on the way of the cross. Who can describe the anguish there must have been in their two hearts at that moment? Then came the fifth sword of sorrow: standing below the cross and seeing Jesus dying in such utter pain and degradation. Imagine a mother seeing her own child suffer such extreme torture but feeling no bitterness, no hatred, no revenge toward those who were taking his life. Mary accepted the death of her Son as Jesus himself had accepted it—as the will of the Father for the salvation of the world! She accepted it because she loved you and me with Christ, her Son. For this she is called the Mother of Sorrows.

The sixth of Mary's sorrows came when Jesus was taken down from the cross and placed in her arms, a scene beautifully rendered in the *Pietà* by Michelangelo. And finally, Mary experienced her seventh sorrow when Jesus' body was placed in the tomb.

These sorrows are a reminder that Mary, the Mother of Mercy, was not spared sorrow in her own life. She knows how to be compassionate to her children. She is with us, especially in our sorrows. Don't we sometimes think that when we are experiencing sorrow, that is when she is furthest away? But those are exactly the times when she is actually closest to us, because she knows what we are going through. We should never doubt her compassion and powerful intercession in our time of need.

No doubt Mary is now constantly before her Son in heaven, taking to him all the needs of her children on earth. Even in the splendor of heaven's glory, she has not forgotten or abandoned her children in this "valley of tears" (from the Salve Regina). Her words to St. Juan Diego in her final apparition to him on December 12, 1531, sum up her sentiments perfectly: "Listen, put it into your heart, my youngest and dearest son, . . . do not let your heart be disturbed. Do not fear this . . . sickness, nor anything that is sharp or hurtful. Am I not here, who am your mother? Are you not under my shadow and protection? Am I not the source of your joy? Are you not in the hollow of my mantle, in the crossing of my arms? Do you need anything more?"[14]

MARY SHOWS US HOW TO BE COMPASSIONATE

So how can we follow Mary's example of compassion? First, we can forgive the injuries done to us. The Lord's Prayer includes the very important petition "Forgive us our trespasses as we forgive those who trespass against us." Our trespasses are our sins and our daily shortcomings. In the Sermon on the Mount, Jesus tells us very clearly, "Do not judge, and you will not be judged; do not condemn, and you will not be condemned. Forgive, and you will be forgiven; give, and it will be given to you . . . ; for the measure you give will be the measure you get back" (Luke 6:37-38).

We have to make a distinction between the sin and the sinner. We can condemn a sin. Jesus himself told the woman who had been caught in adultery not to commit this sin again, but he did not condemn the sinner. He said to her, "I will not condemn you— go in peace" (see John 8:11). So we can condemn the wrong, but we can't condemn the person who does the wrong, because only God knows each person's heart—even the heart of the sinner. Let God judge the person. If we do not condemn the person (though we may have to condemn his actions), God will not condemn us. God will be as merciful to us as we are merciful to others.

Rather than condemn others, we should help those who are trapped in sin. When the Pharisees looked at people who didn't observe the law, they condemned them with a harshness indicating that they couldn't see them as anything but sinners. When Jesus looked at these same people, he saw the potential of great saints. He didn't have a condemning spirit. Rather, with great compassion in his heart, he reached out to sinners, calling them to salvation: "I came that they may have life, and have it abundantly" (John 10:10).

Like Jesus, we must help those who are trapped in sin. We can encourage them to live good lives by our good example. Sometimes that's all it takes! Seeing someone act with kindness can motivate another person to imitate that kindness and do good deeds to others. Encourage people to get back to church, to the sacraments. If they seem nervous, afraid, or fainthearted, encourage them. If they are doubtful or don't know their faith, instruct them. Give them a few pointers on what to do, and above all, pray for them.

MARY REMINDS US TO PRAY
FOR THE CONVERSION OF SINNERS

Our Lady, who is always praying for sinners, asks us to pray for their conversion too. Since my childhood I've been very dedicated to Our Lady of Fatima. Her message to little Lucia, Francesco, and Jacinta has left its imprint on my life. During one of her apparitions, the three children were given a vision of hell. It was absolutely frightening! Afterward, Our Lady said with great sadness in her voice, "You have seen hell, where the souls of poor sinners go! To save them, God wishes to establish in the world devotion to my Immaculate Heart." In another apparition, Our Lady said, "Many souls go to hell because there are none to sacrifice themselves and pray for them."[15] If you study the apparitions of Our Lady, you'll see that every one includes a message to pray for sinners.

For whatever his reasons, our Lord has asked for our cooperation with him for the salvation of souls. He needs our prayers, our good works, and our sacrifices so that people who are far from him, who are hardened in sin—even enemies of the Church or people who may hate God and his Blessed Mother—may someday become great saints.

Do you want a perfect example? A man named Saul of Tarsus was in charge of the stoning of the first martyr of the Church, St. Stephen, and yet he became the great apostle St. Paul. St. Augustine said it was the dying words of that martyr that won the grace of conversion for St. Paul. What did St. Stephen pray? "Lord, do not hold this sin against them" (Acts 7:60).

How about an example closer to our own time? About a hundred years ago, a twelve-year-old girl, Maria Goretti, resisted the sexual advances of a young man named Alexander Serenelli. When she did so, he stabbed her fourteen times. As she lay dying in the hospital, moments before she received Holy Communion, she looked up at a crucifix and prayed, "Lord, I forgive Alexander," and ask God to have mercy on him. Alexander was sentenced to many years in prison. For the first few years, he was very bitter and angry. But then Maria appeared to him in a dream, handing him a bouquet of lilies. In the dream, she told Alexander that she had forgiven him and that she prayed to God that he would be near her in heaven.

Subsequently Alexander had a dramatic conversion. When he was released from prison, a few years early because of his transformation, he went to the home of Maria's mother and asked for her forgiveness. For several years after that, he lived at a Capuchin monastery in Italy doing penance for his sins.

A third example is found in the life of someone who was very devoted to Our Lady—St. Thérèse of Lisieux. When she was fourteen years old, she started to feel the desire to pray for sinners. At the same time, she heard about a man named Henri Pranzini, who was condemned to death and did not want to see a priest. He would not go to confession, even though he was going to die in just a few days. Thérèse began to pray. She offered little sacrifices to God. She even had Mass offered for Pranzini's conversion. She was confident that the Lord would convert him, and she prayed that God would give her some sign for her "own simple consolation."

The day after the execution, she read in a newspaper that the condemned man had resisted almost to the very end but, at the last moment, he grabbed the priest's crucifix and kissed it three times. St. Thérèse took that as a sign that Pranzini had been given the grace of conversion at the last moment and that God had heard her prayers and accepted her sacrifices. "I had obtained the 'sign' I had requested," she wrote, "and this sign was a perfect replica of the grace Jesus had given me when he attracted me to pray for sinners."[16]

Our Lady always reminds us to pray that the grace of conversion might be given to all so that no one will be lost. At Fatima she said that if enough people heeded her message of prayer, penance, and faithful Christian living, then many souls would be saved, atheistic Russia would be converted, and an era of peace would be given to the world. It was the Mother of Mercy who came to remind us so powerfully of this need to pray for God's mercy on sinners.

So let us always pray for the conversion of sinners, remembering the plural "us" in the words we offer daily to Our Lady: "Holy Mary, Mother of God, pray for *us* sinners now and at the hour of our death." God will then open the floodgates of his mercy to all of us through the hands of the Mother of Mercy.

CHAPTER 9

Mary Helps Us Trust Completely in God's Mercy

We need to be able to tell Jesus that we trust completely in his mercy. This is the essential message of the Divine Mercy devotion. Jesus told St. Faustina, "I have opened My Heart as a living fountain of mercy. Let all souls draw life from it. Let them approach this sea of mercy with great trust."[17] And that is why our Lord asked St. Faustina to have inscribed at the bottom of the image of Divine Mercy the words "Jesus, I trust in you." We also need to trust Jesus' mother as dispenser of his mercy. In fact, we can trust Mary to always answer our prayers, bringing them before her divine Son.

One of my favorite prayers is the Memorare, which has been used for hundreds of years by millions of people to seek the Blessed Mother's help. When Our Lady hears the first sentence of that beautiful prayer (see sidebar on next page), do you think that she can ever turn a deaf ear? What confidence is shown in those words! What trust!

And that is the way we should always approach the Mother of Mercy. Don't assume that your prayer hasn't been heard if

The Memorare

Remember, O most gracious Virgin Mary, that never was it known that anyone who fled to your protection, implored your help, or sought your intercession was left unaided. Inspired by this confidence, I fly unto you, O Virgin of Virgins, my Mother! To you do I come; before you I stand, sinful and sorrowful. O Mother of the Word Incarnate, despise not my petition, but in your mercy hear and answer me. Amen.

nothing seems to happen right away. If you don't get an immediate answer to your prayer, you will not be the first one who had to keep knocking persistently. You may have to keep asking a number of times or seeking for a while! I have learned this myself from my own experience. It is also confirmed in the life stories of two great saints.

MOTHER TERESA OF CALCUTTA

Let us start with Mother Teresa of Calcutta. She gave me my greatest earthly possession: a set of rosary beads I always carry with me. It is a simple rosary, made from little beads that grow in India. These beads are popularly called "Job's tears" because every bead looks like a little teardrop. This rosary is so precious to me because it was given to me by someone I knew would someday be a saint. At the time I first met Mother Teresa, I was teaching a group of her sisters in the South Bronx. I will never forget Mother Teresa's words to me as she put the beads in my hands. She thanked me for teaching her sisters and said, "You know that the Blessed Mother is everywhere bringing people to her Son." Then she shared a great secret of the Missionaries of Charity. She told me that when the sisters needed something in a hurry, they prayed the "flying novena." This flying novena consists of saying the Memorare nine times in a row. Compared to traveling long distances by ground transportation, flying gets you there a whole lot faster and more directly. Mother Teresa knew full well the power of Our Lady's intercession with her divine Son. Trying to pray on our own is like using ground transportation; seeking Our Lady's intercession is the spiritual equivalent of flying.

Mother Teresa then related an incident she was involved with that clearly showed the effectiveness of the flying novena. She said that the Missionaries of Charity had a convent in East Berlin, which was then under Communist control. The superior there had become quite ill. Mother Teresa said to me,

Father, I had to remove her and send her back to India. I had to replace her. But because East Berlin was in a very difficult situation, especially dealing with the Communists, not just any sister could handle the situation. I had to bring in a capable sister from India. This meant I needed a visa, but a government official was telling us we would have to wait six months to process this visa. So I gathered the sisters together, and we started to pray the "flying novena"—nine Memorares in a row! When we got to the eighth Memorare, the phone rang. It was a government official telling us again that we would have to wait six months for the visa.

The sisters kept praying. When they finished the ninth Memorare, Mother Teresa spoke to Our Lady more informally. "Mary, we just got done thanking you for obtaining this favor for us, but you didn't, so we are going to ask you again." And she immediately started another nine Memorares. She got to the eighth Memorare the second time through, and the phone rang again. It was another government official, informing her that she could have the visa immediately!

Isn't that the faith that moves mountains? In her time of need, where did Mother Teresa go? To the intercession of the Mother of Mercy: "Remember, O most gracious Virgin Mary, that never was it known that anyone who fled to your protection, implored your help, or sought your intercession was left unaided."

Mary is truly a mother who hears the pleas of all her children. When we cry out in prayer to Mary, her motherly ear—her motherly heart—is always listening.

ST. FRANCIS OF ASSISI

We can see another beautiful example of Mary's hearing the prayers of her children in the life of St. Francis of Assisi. I love my Franciscan vocation. Being a follower of "the little poor man of Assisi," as St. Francis was called in his own lifetime, I've tried to study and absorb his life story. If you are familiar with it, you know that as a young man he wanted to be a knight. To try to fulfill his knightly ambition, Francis headed off to war. On the way, he fell ill. Camping out one night near the city of Spoletto, God spoke to Francis in a dream.

"Francis, where are you going?" God asked.

He answered, "Lord, I am going off to war."

The Lord responded with a second question: "Francis, who can do more for you, the lord or the servant? A rich man or a poor man?"

Francis said, "Of course, the lord can! The rich man can!"

Our Lord asked yet another question: "Francis, then why are you leaving the lord for the servant, a rich man for a poor man?"

Francis immediately grasped the full meaning of Jesus' words: no one could do more for him than Jesus could! So Francis asked what is probably the most important question any of us could ever ask: "Lord, what would you have me do?"[18]

The Lord didn't answer him with a whole plan at that point. When we begin to follow Christ, he usually does not make known everything that we are to do throughout the whole of our lives. He usually reveals these things to us only gradually. So our Lord said simply to Francis, "Go back to Assisi, and there you'll be told what to do."

Francis didn't waste any time fulfilling the Lord's command. Very early the next morning, he returned home. But God didn't seem to be in any hurry to tell Francis what he wanted him to do. Sometimes we forget that God has all eternity at his disposal. God revealed to Francis what he was to do only bit by bit. For example, one day Francis was praying before a crucifix in the little dilapidated chapel of St. Damian. Jesus spoke to him from the cross: "Francis, repair my house which, as you see, is falling into ruin."[19] The chapel indeed was falling down around him. So Francis must have thought to himself, "Well, this must be the work Jesus wants me to do. I'll repair this little chapel."

After rebuilding St. Damian, he repaired a second chapel in honor of St. Peter. Then he went to a third chapel dedicated to Our Lady. It was called St. Mary of the Angels, because it was said that Our Lady and the angels often visited this humble little building. It was also referred to by the popular title "Little Portion" because of its poverty and humility. It was while he was repairing this third chapel that God revealed to him the full understanding of what his real life's work would be.

Francis made the chapel of St. Mary of the Angels a headquarters of sorts, living in a small dwelling nearby. However, he felt that there was still something more that Jesus wanted of him. By now it had been about two years since the Lord said to him, "I'll tell you what to do." Even though Francis had been seeking to know the will of God, his prayer had not been fully answered yet. So what did he do? He made Mary his advocate.

This is how one of his biographers, St. Bonaventure, describes what happened:

> As he was living there in the church of Our Lady, Francis prayed to her who had conceived the Word full of grace and truth, begging her insistently and with tears to become his advocate.[20]

In other words, he went to Mary, and he poured his whole heart out. Then his earnest prayer was answered:

> Then he was granted the true spirit of the gospel by the intercession of the Mother of Mercy and he brought it to fruition. He was at Mass one day on the feast of one of the apostles and the passage of the gospel where our Lord sends out his disciples to preach and tells them how they are to live according to the gospel was read. When Francis heard they were not to provide gold or silver or copper to fill their purses, that they were not to have a wallet for the journey or a second coat, no shoes or staff, he was overjoyed [see Matthew 10:5-10; Luke 10:1-4].[21]

When the Mass was over, Francis asked the priest what the meaning of this gospel passage was. The priest told him that it was about the apostolic life, and that if he wanted to live like the apostles, this is what he had to do. He should not carry any money but have only one simple tunic and go about preaching the gospel. Francis accepted the call. "This is what I want; . . . this is what I long for with all of my heart."[22] He had finally found his vocation: Jesus wanted him to live the apostolic life of the gospels. Through the intercession of Our Lady, in a little chapel dedicated to her, Francis received the answer to his prayers. And we too will receive the answer to our prayers through the intercession of Mary, the Mother of Mercy, when we make her our advocate as well.

St. Bernard (d. 1153) wrote these words about Our Lady that are just as important today as they were over nine hundred years ago:

In danger, in peril, in every hazardous issue, think of Mary, call upon Mary. Keep her name on your lips, keep it in your heart. And that you may secure her help as your advocate, cease not to follow the example of her life.[23]

Endnotes

1. An antiphon from the Office of the Passion.

2. St. Aelred of Rievaulx, Sermon 20 on the Nativity of Blessed Mary as quoted in the Liturgy of the Hours, Volume III, Common of the Blessed Virgin Mary, Office of Readings, 1623–24.

3. http://www.ewtn.com/library/papaldoc/jp2bvm63.htm.

4. Mass in the Shrine of Our Lady of Fatima, May 13, 1982, at www.vatican/va/holy_father/john_paul_ii/homilies/1982/index.htm.

5. http://www.vatican.va/spirit/documents/spirit_20001208_agostino_en.html.

6. http://www.americanrhetoric.com/speeches/fdrfirstinaugural.html.

7. http://www.sacred-texts.com/chr/wosf/wosf03.htm.

8. http://poetry.elcore.net/HoundOfHeavenInRtT.html.

9. The Revelation of Divine Love 68, www.julianofnorwich.org/visions.shtml.

10. Prayer of St. Pio of Pietrecelcina after Holy Communion at www.padrepiodevotions.org/index.asp?pagename=prayers.

11. http://prayers-and-poetry.blogspot.com/2007/06/trust-him-pray.html.

12. Newman Reader–Meditations and Devotions–Part 3. Meditations on Christian Doctrine (299) 1. Hope in God–2. Creator ~March 7, 1848–par. 2–3.

13. http://www.theotokos.org.uk/pages/approved/words/wordguad. html.

14. http://www.theotokos.org.uk/pages/approved/words/wordguad. html.

15. www.theotokos.org.uk/pages/approved/words/wordsfati.html.

16. Story of a Soul, ed. and trans. John Clarke (Washington, DC: ICS Publications, 1976).

17. Diary of St. Maria Faustina Kowalska: Divine Mercy in My Soul (Stockbridge, MA: Marians of the Immaculate Conception, 1987), 1520.

18. www.franciscanfriars.com/vocations/biography2.htm.

19. Ibid.

20. St. Bonaventure, Major Life of St. Francis, 3.1.

21. St. Bonaventure, 3.1.

22. St. Bonaventure, 3.1.

23. From a famous Marian sermon found in Leon Cristiani, St. Bernard of Clairvaux (Boston: Pauline Books and Media, 1984), 57–58.